A West Indian Slave

THE HISTORY OF
MARY PRINCE

A West Indian Slave

Related by Herself

Edited with an Introduction by
Moira Ferguson

REVISED EDITION

ANN ARBOR

The University of Michigan Press

A CIP catalog record for this book is available
from the British Library.

Library of Congress Cataloging-in-Publication Data

Prince, Mary.
     The history of Mary Prince : a West Indian slave / related by
herself ; edited with an introduction by Moira Ferguson. — Rev. ed.
     p.   cm.
     Includes bibliographical references.
     ISBN 0-472-08410-0 (pbk. : alk. paper)
     1. Prince, Mary.   2. Fugitive slaves—West Indies—Biography.
3. Slavery—West Indies.   I. Ferguson, Moira.   II. Title.
HT869.P6A3   1997
306.3′62′092—dc21
     [B]   97-37362
                                                                CIP

Acknowledgments

In preparation for this new edition of *The History of Mary Prince*, I spent time in Bermuda. I want to begin by thanking all the many people who welcomed me so warmly there in 1994: the mayor, the governor, the premier, Sir John Swann, Marjorie Bean, O.B.E., and Rosalind Robinson and other members of the Kenneth Ellsworth Robinson family, Jolene Bean, and Meredith Ebbin. I owe a large debt of gratitude to Michelle Gabisi and Sandra Smith Burrows, who helped coordinate the visit, to Arthur Hodgson, who kindly initiated the visit, and most particularly to Sonia Grant, who organized this visit in a most careful and generous way. I also want to thank the faculty, students, and administration of the Berkeley Institute for their excellent hospitality. I extend my grateful appreciation to the sponsors of my visit—the Ministry of Community and Cultural Affairs and the Ministry of Human Affairs and Information—and to the law firm of Richards, Francis, and Francis, especially Arnold Francis. I thank the curator of the Bermuda Archives, John Adams, Karla M. Hayward and Sandra Taylor Rouja, assistant archivists, for their welcome expertise and attentiveness. I also owe a debt of gratitude to the excellent, pioneering scholarship of Cyril Outerbridge Packwood, and to Vernon Jackson for his unstinting scholarly assistance on this project.

I thank Michael Peterman of Trent University, Canada, for valuable information on Susanna Strickland, and the staff of the Moorland-Spingarn Research Center, Howard University, for furnishing documentation on Ashton Warner.

For this second edition, I also spent time in Antigua and warmly thank the following people for their generous hospitality and information. Brenda Lee Brown, St. John's; Louise Hector, St. John's; Mrs. Bridget Harris, archivist, and Mrs. Maudrey Gonzales, assistant archivist, at the Natural Archives; Desmond V. Nicholson, director, Michele Henry, assistant curator, and staff member Kitz Rickert, Museum of Antigua and Barbuda, St. John's, Antigua; the friendly staff of Joe Mikes Hotel, St. John's; and Annie Drew for helping to make my stay so pleasant and productive.

I remain indebted to those who assisted me with the first edition, including Ziggi Alexander, Peter Fryer, Elaine Hobby, Oyekan Owomoyela, and Ron Ramdin for invaluable discussions of the text. I also want to thank numerous staff members of the British Library who aided me in this project. Assistant Archivist Sandra Rouja of the Bermudan Archives, Hamilton, Bermuda, the late curator Helen Rowe, also of the Bermuda Archives, and Nancy Cardwell helped me early on to track down information about Mary Prince's life and owners in Bermuda, and Natalie Porter facilitated my access to this information. I thank all of them warmly. June Tomlinson, senior library assistant at the Institute of Advanced Legal Studies, assisted me in uncovering references to the court cases, and Dulcie Mapondera helped me gain access to this source. I am grateful to Anne Enscott, senior librarian, Mitchell Library, North Road, Glasgow; to Miss G. A. Matheson, keeper of the manuscripts at the John Rylands University Library of Manchester; to its generous staff; to Angela Whitelegge, senior assistant librarian, Goldsmith's Library, University of London, Senate House; and to Mrs. Seton, archivist, Jane Partington, library assistant, and Brian Scott, assistant librarian, from Reader Services of the Methodist Missionary Society Library in the School of Oriental and African Studies, London. All of these individuals generously opened up their collections to me. I thank D. J. Johnson, deputy clerk of the Records, Record Office, House of Lords, London, and the staff of the Public Record Office for supplying documentation. I appreciate the help of Steven Kyle at the University of Nebraska–Lincoln and the assistance of Philippa Brewster and Candida Lacey, my editors for the first edition.

I owe a debt of gratitude to my editor at the University of Michigan Press, LeAnn Fields, and to the staff, for valuable assistance. I also want to thank the staff of the interlibrary loan and circulation departments at the University of Nebraska, especially Brian Zillig, Debra Pearson, and Kate Adams. Finally, I warmly thank Angela Volzke and Kristen James for the typing and preparation of the manuscript; and Marc Krasnowsky for his immeasurable support.

Contents

Introduction to the Revised Edition

THE VOICE OF FREEDOM: MARY PRINCE

On a farm in Brackish Pond, Devonshire Parish, Bermuda, a woman was born about 1788 who would become the first black British woman to escape from slavery. Her name was Mary Prince; her book about her life and experiences, entitled *The History of Mary Prince, a West Indian Slave, Related by Herself,* differs in several important respects (to be discussed subsequently) from other accounts by black female slaves. Much of what we know about Mary Prince comes from this book. The rest we can reconstruct from Bermudian archives, additional historical facts, and conspicuous gaps in her narrative. *The History* was published in London and Edinburgh in 1831 and had gone into a third edition by the end of that year.[1] It contributed a pointed antislavery message to the fierce agitation both for and against slavery that had already stamped the early years of that decade.

In 1828, Mary Prince came into a London steeped in controversy that polarized the nation and incensed the colonists. She was accompanied by a Mr. and Mrs. Wood, typical representatives of the antiemancipationist plantocracy. The facts of her life explain the timeliness of her arrival.

Economic crisis in Britain had scaled new heights by 1830. In all probability, the crisis would have directly affected Mary Prince's life, as well as the lives of the white working class and the 10,000 to 15,000 strong black community, "the great majority [of whom] . . . were very poor indeed and had to fight, in one way or another, to survive."[2] Factories were closing down, unemployment increased rapidly, and "the wages of those still employed fell."[3] From the 1830s to the 1850s "a minimum of 10 per cent of the English population were paupers."[4]

Such social and economic turmoil was the inevitable consequence of a country in the throes of a fundamental economic transformation from a primarily agricultural to an industrial system of production. The abolition of slavery, as C. L. R. James and Eric Williams have compellingly argued, was an integral part of that process of "modern" capital accumulation.[5] According to the 1831 census, half the population was living in urban areas compared to a majority who had lived and worked in agricultural settings only sixteen years earlier.[6] In response to these drastic economic shifts, reform was the talk of the country and the core of two major campaigns: one for electoral reorganization and the other for the abolition of slavery. Abolitionists overwhelmingly outnumbered proslavery advocates. "Between 1826 and 1832 more than 3,500 [antislavery] petitions were submitted to the House of Lords alone."[7] In fact, both houses of Parliament discussed parliamentary reform and emancipation in every session the year that Mary Prince's *History* was published, while in the previous session (1830–31) a motion had been introduced "for measures to promote its [slavery's] abolition . . . and for compensation should it be abolished."[8]

Bermuda, at the time Mary Prince was born, was a self-governing British colony lying about 600 miles from the coast of Virginia in the western North Atlantic ocean. Not one island but an archipelago of seven major and over 150 smaller islands and rocks that encompasses about twenty square miles, "just under [the size] of Manhattan Island,"[9] Bermuda was proclaimed a Crown colony in 1684. Despite its isolation, Bermuda's strategic proximity to important trade routes made it popular with long-distance travelers as a fuel and rest stop. From the time seafarers and shipwrecked British colonists en route to Virginia founded it in the seventeenth century and until Mary Prince's birth, its major industries (aside from smuggling and wartime racketeering) were shipbuilding and salting. Seaworthy cedars covered a third of the island. Turks Island, the focus of the Bermudian salt industry, lies 720 miles south in the remote Caicos group. Lacking good soil and abundant natural resources, Bermuda never became a plantation colony.

In 1788, less than 200 acres of land were being cultivated, and the population numbered between 10,000 and 11,000 people, of whom 5,000 were slaves.[10] The first black people arrived in 1616, sought after for skills much needed in territory that was little more than a haven of "seabirds and swine." They were "the expert divers and sugar cane growers.... Most of these men came from West Indian islands or were seized on board Spanish and Portuguese ships. And early success in agricultural pursuits was due in large measure to skilled blacks."[11] By 1618 it was well known in London colonial circles that there was a sizable black Bermudian population. However, according to Craven, "though the term slave is used as early as 1617, it does not seem to have come into general use for two or three years after" (361).

Later in the seventeenth and eighteenth centuries, descendants of these early black inhabitants organized plots and led revolts that Mary Prince might well have heard about from family members.[12] In her narrative, Mary Prince never explicitly mentions Bermudian slave resistance, an omission that is part of a larger pattern of omissions. Let me explain what I mean.

Mary Prince describes her first twelve years in the home of Captain John Williams Jr. and his wife, Sarah, the daughter of George Darrell, as "the happiest period of my life.... I was made quite a pet of by Miss Betsey [Williams], and loved her very much."[13] Talking now as an adult looking back on her experiences, she immediately follows this remark with a knowing comment about being "too young to understand rightly my condition as a slave."[14]

With this qualification Mary Prince lets the reader know that, had she comprehended her authentic situation at the time, she would have analyzed and described it quite differently. These strategies for encoding the truth and inviting interpretation beyond the surface message are particularly important regarding the question of sexual experiences. Mary Prince's *History* was sponsored by the Antislavery Society, who won public support by detailing atrocities and portraying female slaves as pure, Christlike victims and martyrs in one of their major organs of propaganda, the *Anti-Slavery Reporter.* Women whose cause they sponsored could not be seen to be involved in any situation (even if the women were forcibly coerced) that smacked of sin and moral corruption. Christian purity, for those abolitionists, overrode regard for truth. Mary Prince manages to foil this taboo by encoding her abusive sexual experiences in accounts of angry jealous mistresses and a master who forced her to wash him while he was naked. Mary Prince's difficulty in being able to present her authentic experience stemmed partly from the form that was required. The British female slave narrative did not develop or emerge as part of the British slave narrative genre in the same way as it did in the United States, where "the slave woman . . . [was] a double victim of the two-headed monster of the slavocracy, the lecherous master and the jealous mistress." When black women did write or tell their experiences in the United States, their vivid testimonials frequently focused on sexual exploitation and disruption of family ties.[15] British female slaves and ex-slaves, by contrast, were either written about in the *Anti-Slavery Reporter* or had little or no opportunity to chronicle, let alone publish, their experiences.

Mary Prince's father, whose Christian name was Prince, was jointly owned by Frances and David Trimingham.[16] Worth noting is the fact that Mary Prince's surname is taken from her own father's Christian name. Perhaps this choice indicates a certain self-conscious bonding of family members in the context of white-imposed slavery.

The next stage of her narrative is the sale of Mary Prince and all of her siblings after the death of Sarah Darrell Williams in 1798. Mary Prince was sold for £20 to Captain John Ingham and

Mary Spencer Ingham of Spanish Point.[17] This sale around 1805 formally dissolves any illusions Mary Prince might have held about her situation being "tolerable," especially during the first year with her new owners, referred to in the *History* as Captain I—— and his wife, who lived at Spanish Point, about five miles west of Brackish Pond, on the tip of the main island in the parish of Pembroke.[18] Mary Prince's immediate experiences were gruesome uncoded signals concerning who controls and brutalizes whom.

Mary Prince's initial experience at the Inghams' home signified immediately who was in control and had the right to brutalize others at will. She saw that Hetty, a seemingly indispensable slave, was worked like a cart horse, sadistically abused day and night; ultimately Hetty was in effect murdered.[19] More frightening than that, Mary Prince immediately had to replace Hetty, a dire turn of events that prompted her to run away. When she was returned to Captain Ingham by her father, Mary Prince was emboldened by his paternal presence to charge her owners with rank injustice. How did a seemingly naive twelve year old transform overnight into an acutely aware young teenager? First, the circumstances of her early life had developed her determination. This determination was coupled with a sense of continuing sorrow and anger at deprivation and hardship and the loss of any dignity. In escaping Mary Prince was venting the rage she was compelled to suppress in order to survive. Even temporary escape was a personal catharsis, an active response to powerlessness. A second factor that gave Mary Prince the power to protest her situation was the fact that her family lived not far down the road. Unlike Hetty, who had been pirated from a French ship, probably spoke very little English, and could be arbitrarily maltreated, Mary Prince was a local person who could expose murder, and thus she possessed subtle bargaining power. Third, the rapidity with which she learned tasks and acquired decision-making skills had further bolstered her confidence; so had the solidarity she felt with other slaves. Unlike Africans, who endured kidnapping, the rigors of the Middle Passage, the process of seasoning, and the ordeal of plantation work, she already savored a small measure of independence. Mary Prince, moreover, had learned to milk cows, herd sheep and cattle, rub down horses, feed animals, take care of children, cook for a family, and do all the household chores. By successfully undertaking the work of three people, she forced her employers to appreciate the value of her labor power. Though by no means irreplaceable, she was immeasurably useful.

On the other hand, she came by bitter experience to distinguish different instruments used in floggings. She witnessed the torture of children as well as the murder of postpuerperal Hetty. She endured persistent head punching by her mistress, and once again we can only read between the lines about the reason for the mistress's noxious sadism. Mary Prince's near blindness later in life might well have been caused by these frequent blows. Thus she came to understand the meaning of slavery very concretely, and each experienced event illuminated that reality. She was recognizing her status as a marginalized person, her positioning as an other. Hetty's situation (and Mary Prince's own impatience) fostered qualitative leaps in the latter's awareness. A telling remark about her owners' conduct exhibits her restraint as well as an inimitable flair for language and an aesthetic sensibility, possibly derived from her sawyer father: in Mary Prince's own words, "The stones and timbers were the best things in [their house]; they were not so hard as the hearts of their owners" (54).

Subsequently, she was provoked into running away by her accidental breaking of an already cracked vase and the punishment from both owners that ensued. An earthquake coincided with the end of the master's flogging of a hundred lashes, which took place while she was tied to a ladder.[20] This excessive punishment could also mean that the owners used the broken vase as an excuse to get even with her (in the case of the wife, who was probably seething with jealousy) and to control her (in the case of Captain Ingham, who was probably sexually abusing her). The other slaves extended a moving sympathy but could not intervene—since their own lives were at stake—and only at this point in the narrative does Mary Prince let loose a feeling of overwhelming despair. She recalls that "life was very weak in me, and I wished more than ever to die" (59).

The last-straw incident concerned a cow that wandered off. For this, Captain Ingham struck her in the small of her back as violently as he could, from which she sustained a lifelong injury. Then he proceeded to lash her until she couldn't stand. She fled to her mother's home, which belonged to Captain Darrell, who not long afterward became mayor of Hamilton. In her memoirs, Mary Prince simply identifies Darrell, and quite likely he was kept ignorant of her presence. She might have surmised that her escape to Darrell's house would in some way intimidate Captain Ingham, but her sense of self-preservation would hardly have squared with the white abolitionists' desire to portray innocent, abused victims, nothing more. Certainly the effect of her escape to the house of an upper-class Bermudian politician might have tempered her owner's conduct more than she realized or perhaps as much as she hoped. Mary Prince reports that she "took courage" when her father brought her back. She announced that she "could stand the floggings no longer; that . . . mothers . . . could not save [children] from cruel masters—from the whip, the rope, and the cow-skin." Almost as a spokeswoman for slaves, she referred to her situation as part of the general plight of slaves and went on to report jubilantly: "He did not . . . flog me that day"—a telling statement about Mary Prince's identification with struggle. Resistance had temporarily silenced her predators, if only for a day. She had won, at least in her own mind, a symbolic victory. But she had to endure five more years of "the same harsh treatment" before they sold her to Mr. D—— of Turks Island and Bermuda. Why they sold her when she was still a young, fit, industrious worker is hard to say, but a maintained posture of camouflaged intransigence could explain her early release. Most slaves had only one or two owners in a lifetime, whereas Mary Prince had five before she freed herself. Slaves were frequently purchased for life servitude. A Bermudian governor once stated: "In Bermuda it is thought as reproachful to sell a servant as it would be in my country to sell a son."[21]

Mary Prince eagerly anticipated going to Turks Island, glad to be sprung from the vicious clutches of her owners, although she was forbidden to bid farewell to her family before she embarked. This final act of vengeance on the part of Captain and Mrs. Ingham hints at their buried fury in being unable to bend her (like Hetty) to their will.

The island was a long 720-mile voyage south from Bermuda without adequate food supplies. Henry C. Wilkinson points out that for fifty years "the salt of Turks Island remained the Bermudians' basic commodity with which to acquire their food from America, their clothes in London, or fish in Newfoundland. [They] sent from sixty to seventy-five ships a year . . . and at times perhaps 900 men were spending a part of their time there."²² It was a "second home" for many Bermudians, although by the time Mary Prince went there to work, the salt industry was declining. That decline spelled economic disaster for the archipelago, for salt was the only cash product that Bermudians could trade.

The passengers' near-starvation during the four-week journey to Turks Island about 1805 was an omen of plights to come. After she landed at the Grand Quay, a small town on a sandbank, Mary Prince's new owner sent her to be appraised, seemingly a matter of custom. She was valued at one hundred pounds Bermudian currency, almost double what she had been sold for five or six years earlier.²³ Soon she discovered what Captain and Mrs. Ingham must have known, that conditions of employment on Turks Island were ghastly even by their standards and that Mr. D——was a cold-blooded taskmaster.²⁴ In this even more isolated spot, intolerable working conditions in the old ponds and submission to D——'s authority were the core of her physical existence.

It was all Mary Prince could do to survive, as she rapidly discovered that D——was an excessively composed version of Captain and Mrs. Ingham. Repeatedly he ordered her to be stripped naked, hung up by her wrists, and beaten. During these assaults, he walked by contemplatively, "taking snuff," as Mary

Prince explains, "with the greatest composure" (62). She characterizes life on Turks Island as "sick or well, it was work — work —work!" For a second time, she witnessed murders committed with an arrogant nonchalance and no fear of reprisals. When she tells how the master's son murdered the "little old woman," Sarah, she asserts, for the first time explicitly, her solidarity with other slaves: "In telling my own sorrows, I cannot pass by those of my fellow-slaves—for when I think of my own griefs, I remember theirs." (This championing of the liberation of other slaves is a constant motif in nineteenth-century North American slave narratives.)²⁵ At the same time, exposing her agony also exposes her vulnerable interior that is so frequently barricaded from the reader. Her internal resistance to abuse and confinement from about 1805 to 1810 found little outlet. Life with D——was a harsh affair.

Mary Prince's return to Bermuda about 1810 marked the beginning of another stage in her life, following her early experiences and then her years with Captain and Mrs. Ingham and with D——. Back in Bermuda, Mary Prince cared for D——'s daughters but also had to work "in the grounds." This mandated chore substantially influenced her future because the cultivation and sale of crops were the means by which many slaves earned an income and purchased a modicum of self-sufficiency. A few eventually gained independence.²⁶ No doubt Mary Prince maneuvered her work responsibilities with a view to her own benefit. She planted and hoed, and in addition was responsible for the household and for animal husbandry. She began to save for manumission. Again Mary Prince manifested her capabilities, but by this time she could gauge more shrewdly the value of her labor power than she could fifteen years earlier. This heightened sense of self-worth parallels her unflinching courage on one occasion in defending Miss D—— during one of D——'s habitual drunken beatings. When he savagely sought vengeance against her, she boldly reminded him: "Sir, this is not Turks Island." Mary Prince's courageous action earned her community praise and further fortified her. Once again her self-selected role as an activist and a spokeswoman consciously sites her at the edge of acceptable slave behavior and discourse. The fact that she exploded at D——'s viciousness back home but not on Turks Island spotlights her sense and patience. She had held on, biding her time on Turks Island, a victim of D——'s callous unilateral rule, anticipating an opportunity to free herself. The Turks Island black inhabitants undoubtedly encouraged her opposition, for she mentions some islanders who came to Bermuda after she returned there. They told her about the destruction of a makeshift prayer shed back on the island. The story intimates that slaves on Turks Island had been trying to organize a separate space for themselves. Even more importantly, talk of freedom abounded on the island, for it lay only 200 miles from San Domingo, a free republic after the successful revolution in 1791 by slaves led by Toussaint L'Ouverture and his allies. Slaves from Turks Island frequently escaped to San Domingo.[27]

In D——'s household, moreover, she finally refused to accommodate his licentious whims. His persistent demand that she wash him while he was naked in the bathtub had too long offended her. She put her foot down. When he threatened her, she kept rejecting him. This episode broaches that concealed area of Mary Prince's life taken up with sexual abuse and harassment. This incident is probably the only sexual one that her editor would permit to be published or the only one Mary Prince herself deemed acceptable to narrate because she could publicize overtly her manifest noncooperation. Although she never mentions sexual activity on Turks Island, it could explain why D—— did not leave her behind when he decided to return and leave the business in his son's hands. Instead he brought her back to Bermuda with him, ostensibly as a servant to his daughters. It might also explain why he seems to have permitted her a certain latitude with respect to her family; while she lived on Turks Island, her mother and youngest sister were sent there from Bermuda to work. When they first arrived Mary Prince kept her four-year-old sister, Rebecca, with her for a week.

Viewing the narrative from this perspective enables us to see that Mary Prince repeated in a different way with D—— her earlier conduct toward Captain and Mrs. I——: she worked capably, complied, and sometimes complained, but she never completely knuckled under.[28] Given Mary Prince's economic dependence and the fact that her narrative was intended as propaganda for the antislavery campaign, she would presumably have constructed what she wanted to say very carefully in accordance with what she knew of the aims of the Anti-Slavery Society. In London in 1827, when she escaped, she was employed as a domestic servant by Thomas Pringle, the Methodist secretary of the Anti-Slavery Society and the editor of her *History*. Pringle's friend Susanna Strickland, recently a Methodist convert, had transcribed Mary Prince's narrative while she lived as a guest in Pringle's home sometime during 1829 or 1830.[29] In numerous senses Mary Prince's hands were tied.

At any rate, in relating her break with D——, she explains, "I thought it was high time to do so. After that, I was hired to work [as a washerwoman] at Cedar Hills, and every Saturday night I paid the money to my master."[30] Besides what was owed to D——, she earned twenty pence a day or two dollars and a quarter a week. Perhaps, like Captain and Mrs. Ingham before him, D—— had decided not to wrestle any longer with Prince's resolute spirit, especially now that his barbarities could not be perpetrated with the impunity that the isolation of Turks Island permitted. The fact that Mary Prince self-consciously exploited her earning power to her financial advantage during the years she worked for D—— after her return to Bermuda signifies her personal development as she journeyed to freedom.

She now negotiated the fourth and last step in her life as a slave, requesting D—— to sell her to a Bermudian merchant named John Wood, who was moving to Antigua. "The truth is," she explains to Susanna Strickland, who was transcribing Mary Prince's narrative, "I did not wish to be any longer the slave of my indecent master." Here she directly attacks the "loose" sexuality that evangelicals like Susanna Strickland and Thomas Pringle so ardently deplored and elevates the idea of pure "womanhood" they so vigorously advocated. There were additional reasons why she opted to move. In Turks Island and Bermuda, Mary Prince had become aware of opportunities for employment on other islands. By 1814 or so when she was thinking about how she could leave D——'s household, Mary Prince must also have known that separation from her biological family was well-nigh irrevocable. While she was at Turks Island, her father, Prince, had died. Her seven brothers and three sisters were so dispersed that she knew only the approximate whereabouts of two sisters. Her eldest sister lived in Trinidad, the mistress of her master and mother of his three children. Young Rebecca, whom Prince had entertained on Turks Island, had returned to Bermuda. Given these family circumstances, little remained to hold her in Bermuda, and much remained to escape from. Knowledge of the possible permanence of her position as well as her involuntary alienation from family members seems to have psychologically energized her to plan for freedom. Resourcefulness and a disciplined inner strength aided her efforts.

Besides, Antigua was the most attractive island for any slave actively thinking of freedom. Free black men were permitted to vote there, and, although this law did not apply to Mary Prince, its relative liberality in the Caribbean islands was symbolically significant.[31] More than an expansion of the franchise, the law implicitly recognized that all slaves were potentially entitled to civil rights. The franchise weakened owner control.

In soliciting D—— to sell her to John Wood, Mary Prince used her labor power as her bargaining tool. To begin with, the Woods were reluctant until Mrs. Wood heard of Mary Prince's reputation as a hard worker. For a nursemaid, housekeeper, and washerwoman rolled into one, they paid one hundred pounds. This meant that D—— had utilized Mary Prince's labor without cost to himself for a decade and had even extracted a small profit at the end, not to mention his acts of sexual abuse. Mary Prince might have recognized this exploitation, but more pointedly she would have recognized that her "market value" had not increased except in relation to the cost of living. Age and physical battering had exacted their toll. But her cognizance of economic realities also spurred her plans for self-determination.

In the Antiguan section of the narrative, Mary Prince concentrates on four issues: illness, religion, marriage, and her relationship with the Woods, complicated by her efforts to be free. She begins with her work-related illness because it initially dominated her life and fractured any hope of harmony with her new owners. Paradoxically, her experience as a washerwoman was her undoing *and* her ticket to freedom. She was used to tepid saltwater, and washing clothes for the Woods with cold Antiguan water played havoc with her constitution and crippled her. "For several months," she confides, "I could not lift the [left] limb." Unable to work, she stayed in her only available shelter, a vermin-ridden outhouse.

The Woods were extremely vexed at what they saw as Mary Prince's sabotage of their plan to exploit her to the maximum extent. She had temporarily foiled their efforts to load her down immediately with massive piles of washing, in addition to other major duties. The start of Mary Prince's employment, then, precipitated a power struggle because she no longer accepted her status as a slave. How much of Mary Prince's illness was feigned is impossible to judge, although it is certain—as none other than a plantocratic doctor was to testify later—that she suffered from St. Anthony's fire, an unfeignable illness. St. Anthony's fire or erysipelas results in well-demarcated, slightly raised red areas with advancing borders, usually accompanied by constitutional symptoms. She also suffered from an exceedingly painful form of rheumatism. But it is conceivable that she exaggerated her ill health to assert the only form of power that lay at her disposal— that of her labor. She also could not admit to pretense— feigning—for lying would be anathema to Pringle. The need for slave narratives to double as moral testimony would have mattered more to him than any subversive declaration of independence on Mary Prince's part. She also expressed extreme anger toward Martha Wilcox, the black overseer who lived with the Woods, because Wilcox's free status was the very one that Mary

Prince sought. Having heard Wilcox's complaints, Mrs. Wood threatened to have Mary Prince flogged, but this unity of mistress and domestic overseer failed to daunt her.

Her fiery spirit was even more evident when Mrs. Wood sent her to a magistrate over an incident with a pig. As punishment, she was locked up in the "cage," described by a contemporary as a "cruel practice . . . very common in Antigua." Even one of the magistrates, James Scotland, refused to sanction it (100). After release from this cramped confinement, she was flogged. Two factors unvoiced in the narrative might have exacerbated the series of altercations between Mary Prince and Mrs. Wood. The first was the fact that all of Mrs. Wood's privileges as a white slave-owning wife were embodied in the work designated for Mary Prince. Delegating work and responsibilities and enjoying leisure were among the few forms of power and control that Mrs. Wood possessed. A refusal to work, therefore, became a personal affront, an assault on her power. Second, Mrs. Wood surely harbored sexual jealousy toward Mary Prince. Mr. Wood would have customarily viewed Mary Prince (and other female slaves) as his sexual property. Hence Mary Prince's seven-year affair with a white Captain Abbott and her negotiations to entertain male guests at home after "curfew" would have infuriated both the Woods, but for different reasons. Mary Prince for her part might have viewed a white lover as sexual self-expression and a form of control over her circumstances.[32] Once again, this is an issue more overtly discussed in later African American slave narratives and censored in Mary Prince's text by Pringle or even by Mary Prince herself, in recognition of Pringle's desire to launder or morally and psychologically simplify the *History*. The fact that children are never mentioned—highly unusual in a female slave narrative—raises the question, understandably not mentioned by Mary Prince (or permitted to be mentioned by Pringle)—of possible physical abuse leading to sterilization. Mary Prince's severely weakened health, testified to by Pringle and by a number of writers in the preface to the third edition and in the postscript, as well as by Mary Prince herself, buttresses this speculation.

Mary Prince writes distinctively here and at other points of high tension when she records the direct speech of herself and others. Often she relates nerve-racking experiences in flat understated tones—the scene when the Woods want to load her down in London with vast amounts of washing is one example. But when she reports specific conversations, she brings brief domestic encounters to life with terse but supple phrasing, suggesting someone with a gift for vivid description who has had her oral narrative somewhat toned down for her audience. Nonetheless, it always bears the hallmark of internal suffering, of mental as well as physical torture. She subtly suggests her daily vulnerability to sexual harassment. In the final persuasive oration, Mary Prince's lively style of speech comes into its own. In addition, the proslavery advocates (one of whom baptized her) query only the intensity of the cruelty she alleges, never the account itself. That alone seems irrefutable testimony, alongside the innumerable references to esoteric facts about slave conditions and day-to-day West Indian life continually mentioned by Mary Prince, and repeated by her in court under oath. In the final persuasive oration Mary Prince comes into her own. Let me cite a few examples: "Poor child, poor child . . . You must keep a good heart, if you are to live here," sorrowful slaves advised her when she arrived at the Inghams' house. After she broke the ornament at the Inghams' home, she woefully exclaimed, "O mistress, the jar has come in two," accurately anticipating a harsh reaction, her emotion evident in the blurting succinct appeal. During her miserable years at Turks Island, she reports no conversation with D——. She only records "Sir, this is not Turks Island" in her moment of triumph back in Bermuda. She mentions one other conversation, in shock after seeing her mother's confusion on Turks Island: "Mammy, is this you? . . . Mammy, what's the matter?" Her anxious repetitions draw the reader close. So does her taut report of Mrs. Wood's sadistic taunt: "You have been used to the whip . . . and you shall have it here." She also records in direct speech Mr. Burchall's offer to purchase her: "If you intend to sell her, I may as well buy her as another." Further direct statements come from her husband, Daniel James: "Sir, I am a free man, and thought I had a right to choose a wife." After she asks to be manumitted, she enrages Mrs. Wood by reminding her in cool tones that "to be free is very sweet." This last statement and one other exemplify a careful self-vindication: she tells Mrs. Pell why leaving the Woods is justified: "I can stay no longer to be used"; their supposedly sotto voce rejoinder exposes their manipulative wicked ways: "If she goes the people will rob her, and then turn her adrift." But last we have Mary Prince's understated exultation before departure, her mind made up: "I always worked very hard to please them, both by night and day; but there was no giving satisfaction."

Irate at Mary Prince's obduracy, Mrs. Wood persistently plagued her rheumatoid worker with complaints about her job performance while simultaneously inundating her weekly with undue amounts of washing. Finally, Mary Prince refused: "At last my heart was quite full, and I told her that she ought not to use me so." (This speech echoes her plucky reprimand to Captain and Mrs. Ingham over a decade earlier when her father returned her after she ran away.) Mary Prince then heaped blame on an already enraged Mrs. Wood for her miserable isolation in the outhouse. Such calculated audacity reaped a rewarding harvest. The Woods acted precisely as Mary Prince ideally desired. The incident indirectly informs us what Prince sought but could not secure from Captain Ingham. The Woods told her to find a new owner, and she did. Then they reneged, and Mr. Wood whipped her. But a pattern had been established that continued even when all three traveled to London around 1828. They expressed dissatisfaction, ordered her to go, and then declined to sell her. I will return to their seemingly erratic behavior in a moment.

During these wranglings, at least three men offered to negotiate for Mary Prince with a view to her eventual manumission: Adam White, a free black artisan, a Mr. Burchell, and Captain Abbott.[33] The Woods refused each one. Additionally, Mrs. Wood sold five other slaves in Antigua while she employed the recalcitrant Mary Prince. Any action by Mary Prince to establish autonomy was intensely counteracted by the Woods. Or so it seemed. For example, when she married a pious, hard-working, free black widower named Daniel James in December 1826 at Spring Gardens in St. Johns, the Woods worked themselves up so much that Mrs. Wood compelled Mr. Wood to flog Mary Prince with a horsewhip. "I thought it very hard to be whipped at my time of life for getting a husband—I told her so." Mary Prince had disempowered them by an autonomous (and irreversible) decision. Subsequently, Mrs. Wood forbade Daniel James's clothes to be washed in her tub, symptomatic of her inability to cope with or be reminded of a sexually active and self-reliant slave wife.

All this might suggest that the Woods disliked Mary Prince, but the facts relay a different story. She was their special confidential servant who was entrusted with care of the house when they left for extended periods. Mary Prince took full advantage of their trust to stake out a path to freedom. Her careful grooming and some free exercise of her sexuality enhanced this evident self-possession. Primarily while the Woods were gone, she sold coffee, yams, and other provisions to ships' captains and bought hogs at the dock to sell for double the amount on shore. She washed clothes for money. Shrewd and painstaking, she reached the point where she could financially negotiate her manumission. The dramatic reaction of the Woods to Mary Prince's bid to buy her freedom seems predictably irrational: "Mrs. Wood was very angry—she grew quite outrageous—she called me a black devil . . . but she took good care to keep me a slave" (75). By precipitating large trauma in the lives of the Woods, Mary Prince quietly wreaked vengeance through sabotage.

The question, of course, arises about the senselessness of the Woods' behavior. The model of a master/slave relationship propounded by G. W. F. Hegel may cue us to what was happening. In his discussion of the psychology of domination and cultural patterns in ancient Greece in *The Phenomenology of Spirit*, Hegel identifies the two important aspects of a slave with respect to the master: the slave's labor and the notion of recognition.[34] By recognition, Hegel means that the existence of the slave depends on the existence of the master. Hegel argues, however, that the moment of revolution comes when the slave recognizes that his or her primary identity lies with the other slaves and as a result withdraws both labor and recognition. At this point when the slave no longer sees his or her identity as necessarily mediated through the master, then not only is the slave not a slave, but the master is not a master.[35] Domination, therefore, depends on the consent of the governed. Mary Prince's situation proves the validity of Hegel's hypothesis. The Woods could not countenance their lack of control over Mary Prince once she recognized and acted upon her entitlement to freedom. What was more, recognizing these contradictions, Mary Prince astutely exploited them and compelled confrontation. With money to buy her freedom, she fearlessly challenged the Woods. The Woods acted absurdly because she undermined their role as slave owners in the community. Retaining their control of Mary Prince symbolized retaining their identity as the master cláss.

In addition, the Woods evaluated Mary Prince's desire to leave them and find another master who would manumit her as a reflection on the quality of their ownership. So they compelled her to remain their slave in order to protect themselves from a moral judgment about the quality of servitude in their household. Thus the spiral built and collapsed. The more the Woods taunted Mary Prince into leaving and the more she negotiated advantageously for a new owner, the more they forced her back, using the law, the only weapon at their disposal. They failed to recognize Mary Prince's goading of their vulnerability, her quiet wreaking of vengeance through sabotage. The Woods entangled themselves in their own net of psychological-political necessity and social self-deception. Nor did the Pringle household, we suspect, recognize the implications of Mary Prince's discourse at this point; they had constructed Mary Prince as a victim, and they were blind to her politics of conscious or unconscious subterranean resistance.

Wider explanations exist, too, for the Woods' irrationality. The bill for full emancipation was being debated in the British

Parliament in the 1820s, while in the country at large, agitation for emancipation approached the peak of its controversy.[36] Ladies' Anti-Slavery Societies mushroomed as press reports from the West Indies about slave resistance multiplied. Proslavery press reporters foamed at the mouth. In denying her owners' power and nullifying their control, Mary Prince identified with freed blacks and with the opposition back home in Bermuda that would eventually aid in the defeat of the Woods and their class. Prince's resistance represented a microcosm of black opposition, an individual expression of the collective consciousness that sought an end to illegitimate domination. In Angela Davis's words, "her routine oppression had to assume an unconcealed dimension of outright counterinsurgency." She participated in what a historian of slavery, Michael Craton, has characterized as "a continuum of active slave resistance."[37] She drove the Woods to know that not only was control diminishing within their household and the risk increasing daily of aspersions being cast against them, but also that the double security of themselves and their plantocratic allies was fundamentally imperiled. Very few, if any, white contemporaries would have discerned such a powerful undercurrent in the autobiography.

Mary Prince devotes almost half of the Antiguan recollections to her religious experiences. Her conversion to Moravianism allied her with other slaves, with free blacks, and with the minority of whites who believed in spiritual equality. Since she had been separated from her family, the idea of being part of another family considerably attracted her. Religion combined resistance, escape, relief, spiritual satisfaction, and an opportunity for wider human connection. For Mary Prince, religion built a bridge to freedom and social acceptance.

Whenever and however she could, Mary Prince fractured every old oppressive bond. The fact that she married soon after conversion further affirms her heightened consciousness, her refusal of the role of slave. As a motif, religion was favored by white abolitionists to attract a white Christian audience to the cause. A slave's conversion affirmed for a white audience the "validity" of their values, their false perception of the inferiority of African values, and the moral bankruptcy of Christian slave owners. With conversion a critical propaganda motif, Mary Prince must have been thoroughly encouraged to display religion as a culminating point to her life as a slave. On her last page she thanks Mrs. Pringle for teaching her "daily to read the word of God . . . [and] the great privilege of being enabled to attend church three times on the Sunday." She ends by thanking the Reverend Mr. Young who has "taken much pains to instruct me" and the Reverend Mr. Mortimer "under whose ministry I have now sat for upwards of twelve months."[38]

Through this virtually mandated discussion of religion and supposed past sins, Mary Prince can offer us one of the few glimpses of her sexual reality, all but suppressed throughout the narrative. She informs us that, after her first church meeting, "I felt sorry for my sins. . . . I cried the whole night, but I was too much ashamed to speak." This probably refers to physical relationships, which were occasionally hinted at. One in particular with Captain Abbott is mentioned later by Joseph Phillips of Antigua, a personal advocate and an abolitionist, the target of much proslavery ridicule both for his opinions and his marriage to a black woman.[39] Moravian doctrine certainly tried to rouse moral guilt, for as Elsa Goveia points out, the Moravians primarily dwelt on "the great practical duties of piety, mercy, justice, temperance, charity, sobriety, industry, veracity, honesty, fidelity, and obedience to their masters." They also stressed "the obligation as Christians, to confine themselves to one wife, and to preserve inviolable fidelity to the marriage bed."[40] In the words of the Methodist John Baxter: "I am in an enemy's country. Women and drink bear down all before them here."[41] Apparently influenced by Moravian ideas and significantly fortified by this newfound support and the degree of social acceptance that resulted, Mary Prince married Daniel James, a cooper, a violin player, and a carpenter like her father, soon afterward, without notifying the Woods in advance. She testified to these personal facts during the trial of *Wood v. Pringle*. Clearly, consciously, and dramatically rebelling against the Woods, she states it flatly in her testimony.

The fifth and last phase in Mary Prince's narrative began when the Woods decided to visit London about 1828 with their son in order to pick up their daughters, and Mary Prince asked to accompany them. In this change of setting she obviously foresaw an opportunity for liberty. "My husband," she explains, "was willing for me to come away, for he had heard that my master would free me."[42] Unfortunately, Daniel James's information did not turn out to be accurate.

Mary Prince found London a nightmare. During the journey from Antigua, her limbs swelled drastically. On their arrival at the Tower of London, Mrs. Wood showed scant sympathy. When they took up residence in Leigh Street, Wood immediately insisted that Mary Prince launder large loads of accumulated bedding and washing from their journey. Even the cook protested; the English washerwomen at the local facilities were shocked by such monstrous behavior toward a partial invalid and did the washing for Mary Prince. The Woods' attitudes forced the substitute washerwoman in their household to leave. All around Mary Prince were people in different capacities openly contemptuous of the Woods. But she well knew that her departure from the Woods' household would cost her much she held dear—her Antiguan connections, her husband, and her family. It would constitute a permanent fracture with her past life. She would also have to contend with rheumatism and finding work in an alien society. Yet her desire for freedom ultimately conquered these reservations as she brought her life as an energetic, steady laborer full circle. In the early years of her brutal enslavement to Captain Ingham and D——, Mary Prince used hard work and ingenuity to order her universe and survive. She learned strategies of survival, both accommodationist and resistant. With the Woods in England, she employed the same ingenuity—what Joseph Phillips has termed her "superior intelligence"—to offer the labor power she felt she was capable of offering rather than what they insisted on. Now Mary Prince undertook work on her own, not on the Woods' terms. Mentally, Mary Prince had reversed her situation, the Woods had become the outsiders because Mary Prince had subtly reconstructed all the aspects of their power relationship, except the legal physical one.

The Woods were as persistent, as conflicting, and as derisive as ever in their attitude toward Mary Prince. Three times in London they baited her into leaving, even to the point of Mr. Wood supplying her with a note granting his permission for her departure. Confident that lack of familiarity with England in addition to illness would deter her, they smugly surmised they would end up teaching her a lesson about domination and dependence. Cultural arrogance, notions about white superiority, insecurity, and suppressed fear had so blinded them to her intelligence and personal heroism that her exit came as a shock. They immediately tried to manipulate her into changing her mind, but when antislavery individuals and agencies assumed Mary Prince's cause, the Woods dug in their heels about selling her. The old pattern reasserted itself. Their reputation as exemplary slave owners was now at stake in public, so any agreement to part with her would be tantamount to accepting moral censure. No form of coercion— economic, moral, or psychological—seemed to work on them. Denying culpability to the bitter end, they left London for Antigua, having successfully prevented a discussion in the House of Commons about their conduct as slave owners, a coup de grâce that their pride and perversity could not allow Mary Prince.[43] But, in spite of them, she did remain behind. They had to abandon their arduous struggle to avoid further embarrassment. In the final battle of wills, Mary Prince won.[44] She had refused to be a blank page, a body and nothing more, on which they inscribed their power. They had used her to define themselves, and they ended up being defined negatively by her, in public, both at home and abroad.

In her memoirs, Mary Prince traces her efforts to survive in London and her eventual meeting with members of the antislavery society.[45] Indomitable, she lent her weight to the parliamentary struggle against slavery, elated at her successful personal bid for freedom. But the posture she adopted was that of a spokeswoman for all. The memories of the slave communities in which she participated motivated her. The freedom of her family was also at issue. She became the first black British spokeswoman for general emancipation, ending her *History* with the public plea on its behalf. Her cadence and rhetorical devices, in sharp contrast to a narrative mainly characterized by understatement, are those of a gifted natural orator. Her collective spirit is manifest to the end.

Whether Mary Prince's *History* was reshaped after she dictated her experiences to Susanna Strickland, and if so, how much, is hard to say, but many aspects of the *History* do conform to fairly conventional propagandistic slave narratives. Those from the nineteenth-century United States, for example, followed a certain development, aspects of which roughly resembled aspects in Prince's narrative. They include biographical data about births and childhood or they explain the lack of such data; they then describe the conditions that provoke attempts at escape and elaborate on the escape itself. The narratives often conclude on an upbeat with the free individual's arrival in the promised land.[46] The salient motifs thus become the fugitive slave, the direct assault on slavery as an institution, and concrete examples of abuse. Popular eighteenth-century British narratives of African-born freedmen such as Ukowsaw Gronniosaw (James Albert) and Olaudah Equiano (that went through, respectively, twelve editions in forty-four years and thirty-six editions in forty-eight years) contrast sharply but also bear resemblance to some aspects of Mary Prince's *History*. These narratives, in contrast to U.S. narratives, dwell on events chronologically, their aim being to instruct readers and encourage humanitarian concerns.[47] Mary Prince's narrative bears some resemblance to both of these formats, but neither the narratives of the African-American fugitive slave nor those of the "high-born African narrator" who does not begin life as a slave exactly reflect her unique account. To be sure, Mary Prince treats life-threatening situations with brave alertness, and assuredly she lives by her wits, sabotaging in a limited fashion where she can, eventually embracing a Christian doctrine that brings some security and coherence into her life.[48]

But there is another dimension to her narrative. The mandatory sections on childhood, brutality, torture and yet more torture fuse with commentary on her fractured family, her religious conversion, a morally responsible marriage, her escape, a pronounced desire to work and to continue receiving religious instruction, and an exhortation to emancipate, aimed at a wide national audience. Jealous mistresses, white owners' cruelty, Mary Prince's honesty, and the taboo on sex and its camouflaged references are further standard features. All of these factors in turn mollify and inflame the public. Unlike many narratives from the United States, Mary Prince's is not a series of hair-raising adventures. Instead—like such eighteenth-century British slaves as Ignatius Sancho, who was born a slave, became a servant of the aristocratic Montagus, and then established himself as a letter writer and a grocer—she walks away, privileged (in one strictly limited sense) by living in Britain.[49]

But more than its resemblance to transatlantic slave narratives, Mary Prince's narrative seems related to the format of cases reported in the *Anti-Slavery Reporter*, the press organ of the Anti-Slavery Society, of which Pringle was secretary. Through the *Reporter* and elsewhere, the cases of such abused and exploited female slaves as Kitty Hylton, Grace Jones, and Kate had become notorious causes célèbres.[50] The *Reporter*'s weekly accounts of such cases usually included details of the legal dispute, authenticating apparatus by eyewitnesses, details of trial testimony, numerous and hideous goings-on and occasional resistance, and some account of abolitionist activity. Mary Prince's narrative and its supplement by Pringle follow this format quite closely, with additional information about childhood customarily found in autobiographical accounts. Her *History*, then, combines aspects of the eighteenth-century British slave narrative, the nineteenth-century U.S. narrative, and the format of recorded court cases of slave abuse. Because of its rarity, Mary Prince's *History* is also sui generis, with no comparable account extant by a female West Indian slave.

Nor is there much to quibble about regarding the authenticity of the narrative, despite its being so transparently pressed into the service of antislavery propaganda and censored by evangelical dictates. It is neither manufactured, in Philip Curtin's phrase, "out of whole cloth," nor is it a well-meaning fraud.[51] New information about her father and her owners incontrovertibly establishes the veracity of her narrative. Pringle's testimony in the preface and footnotes about the authenticity of the narrative seems credible. I have noted Mary Prince's testimony in direct speech that speaks for itself. In addition, the proslavery advocates (one of whom baptized her) query only the intensity of the cruelty she alleges and not the account itself. That seems irrefutable testimony. So are the innumerable references to esoteric facts about slave conditions and day-to-day West Indian life mentioned by Mary Prince, as well as her inimitable diction, in which she reports her mother, for example, lamenting the "shrouding" of her children prior to their sale.

Another new piece of evidence we do have concerns Mary Prince's ability to enjoy social occasions in London. This observation is recorded by Susanna Strickland, who makes the following comment about Mary Prince on the day of Strickland's own wedding. This, apparently the only lighthearted social description in existence of Mary Prince, has just recently come to light:

> St. Pancras Church made the happiest girl on earth, in being united to the beloved being in whom I had long centered all my affections. Mr. Pringle "gave me" away, and Black Mary, who had treated herself with a complete new suit upon the occasion, went on the coach box, to see her dear Missie and Biographer wed.[52]

Since Mary Prince's consciousness, too, must have been conditioned by what happened to her, she may even have cherished this self-representation. Despite her image as a religious moral person, she does end up inverting the traditional paradigm of power. This turning the tables is one of her victories. In summarizing the experience of the "generic" slave, she simultaneously exhibits both her disgust at human predacity and the gutsiness that kept her going. The response she arouses is evident in the statement made about Mary Prince's *Narrative* by the amanuensis, Susanna Strickland.

> I have been writing Mr. Pringle's black Mary's life from her own dictation and for her benefit adhering to her own simple story and language without deviating to the paths of flourish or romance. It is a pathetic little history and is now printing in the form of a pamphlet to be laid before the Houses of Parliament. Of course my name does not appear. Mr. Pringle has added a very interesting appendix and I hope the work will do much good . . . I have given away most of your Prospectuses but I am sorry to say with no success.[53]

The traditional harangue of abolitionist discourse is the exact vehicle, coincidentally, that permits her personality to come alive. She becomes for a moment a compelling street-corner orator. Thus, despite the abolitionists' intention to portray her life as a moral fable in which an individual living in ignorance and harsh conditions attains a God-given freedom through perseverance, conversion, and a constant faith, by the end she radiates as an indomitable self-made heroine.

Mary Prince's history is a model of emotional containment by someone with no consistently safe nurturing environment who is forced to please her advocates by conforming, yet is seething with anger and a sense of repression as she follows orders and acts piously. Obliged to confine herself within the parameters of acceptable debate, Mary Prince undoubtedly encodes her discourse, using all the conventions at her disposal, to plead her unique self. Nonetheless, she elaborates very little on her internal reflections or on her relationships, nor can we know very much how she feels about her public presentation of self in the role of a docile Christian slave-servant, emblematic of virtue.

And finally, in the closing plea to the readers, Mary Prince conveys a sense of dignified exaltation in being enabled, finally, to turn the tables on those who had hitherto wielded a near absolute power over her. Here in a sense is the resolution of her inevitable conflict in trying to say all the right things, of abiding by the prescriptions about how a "female" should act, about determining what an ex-slave should say, yet remaining true to herself.

It would be nice to end by telling how Mary Prince lived the rest of her life free and in comparative comfort and contentment. Unfortunately, no such evidence is available. On the contrary, we know from an addendum to the preface of the third edition that Mary Prince's health was deteriorating. She was going blind. Moreover in 1831, after Prince's employer and editor, Thomas Pringle, secretary of the Anti-Slavery Society, published her *History,* an intense public controversy erupted as to its accuracy. The main participants were Pringle and Mary Prince's antislavery supporters on the one side and the proslavery lobby, headed by the notorious James Macqueen, editor of the *Glasgow Courier* and a sworn foe of emancipation, on the other. The Reverend James Curtin, an Anglican missionary who had baptized Mary Prince into "the English church," was another vocal antiemancipationist who challenged Mary Prince's narrative.[54] Macqueen and Joseph Phillips had previously clashed in public over Phillips's work in aiding "distressed Negroes" in Antigua.[55] Macqueen denied that such men and women existed.

First of all, James Macqueen lashed out at Mary Prince's veracity and railed splenetically about her morals and the morals of Pringle and emancipationists in general. Then two court cases ensued.[56] Clearly Mary Prince had touched a raw public nerve with her unalloyed presentation of one person's experiences. The furor that she raised proves how persuasively she expressed the popular ideology of freedom—anathema to Macqueen and his allies.[57] The public altercation also proved that the subtlety of her implied message had worked its way under the skin of proslavery advocates, who were sensitive to every nuance of expressed black will.

Ironically, both cases were settled in the same year that the Emancipation Bill finally passed the House of Lords—1833. (The exact date of the bill's passage was July 31, 1833.) In the first court case, Pringle sued Thomas Cadell, the publisher of *Blackwood's Magazine,* which published Macqueen's savage diatribe against Mary Prince, Thomas Pringle, and emancipation. This hearing affords us one of the only images we have of Mary Prince outside her narrative. In the words of the court recorder: "At the London Court of Common Pleas, Thursday, February 21st, 1833, before Lord Chief Justice Tindal and a special jury . . . there was an action brought by Thomas Pringle . . . against [the publisher, Thomas Cadell]. Mary Prince was then called in and sworn. She is a negress," the reporter continues, "of very ordinary features and appears to be about thirty-five years of age. She stated that she gave an account of her life to Mr. Pringle. No other question was put to her by the plaintiff's counsel, and the other side declined to cross-examine her."[58] Five days later at the King's Bench, Guildhall, Prince's former owner, John Wood, brought an act for libel against Thomas Pringle. John Wood won by default because Pringle could not produce witnesses from the West Indies to prove his allegations.[59]

That second court case marks the last appearance of Mary Prince, an intrepid woman narrating a pioneering history: the first British black woman to write an autobiography and a polemic against slavery.[60]

Mary Prince testified for some length at that trial and reaffirmed several of the brutalizing incidents from her published *History.* Her testimony in court also confirms that the evangelical editors had censored several accounts of sexual activity from her narrative. Her brushes with the law that she recounts were clearly related to her vulnerability as a slave. That court case marks the last known appearance of Mary Prince, who contributed a distinguished groundbreaking oral narrative to world history.

In summary, Mary Prince inaugurates a black female counter-offensive against a reductive conception of black women as flogged, half-naked victims of slavery's entourage. Her text encourages a view of emancipationist writers based on gender and racial difference. Since no African British female who had been a slave prior to 1831 had written for publication, Mary Prince's narrative helped to name that hitherto untold history and at the same time complicated customary one-sided though politically differentiated accounts by abolitionists and plantocrats alike. Claiming voice and agency, Mary Prince debunks old mythologies, declines external definitions of slaves and ex-slaves, and clears a path for more open contestations of power in the future. She announces her participation not only in the emancipationist and anticolonialist struggles but in the collective movement for black women's rights.

Mary Prince's story calls for a reappraisal of what has been written about black and other racially oppressed women. Her narrative proffers a sense of how psychological trauma, physical torture, and hardship were overcome, as well as some understanding of how legal, economic, and social shackles affected life and the ways in which human beings could use and shape their environment to exercise some control over their own future. Her story is of riveting interest because she highlights not only the suffering and indignities of enslavement but also the triumphs of the human spirit.

NOTES

1. The text was published by F. Westley and A. H. David and also by Waugh and Innes in Edinburgh. Appended is "A Supplement by the Editor" in which Thomas Pringle, secretary of the Anti-Slavery Society, explains the circumstances of his publishing Mary Prince's narrative. He includes testimony from supporters of Mary Prince and mentions detractors. The text went into a third edition that

year. No reviews of the text in such prominent periodicals as the *Athenæum,* the *Critical Review,* the *Monthly Review,* or the *Edinburgh Magazine* were published, probably because the narrative had provoked such immediate controversy. In 1830–31, *Hansard* makes no mention of the *History* either. All references in the text will be to the first edition of Mary Prince's *History.* Versions of the introduction to this text were read at *The Black Woman Writer and the Diaspora Conference,* East Lansing, Michigan, October 27, 1985; the Women's Studies Colloquia Series at the University of Nebraska–Lincoln, November 14, 1985; the Modern Language Association, San Francisco, December, 1987; the University of London History Workshop Colloquium, July, 1988; and the Hamilton Center for Historical Studies, Bermuda, February 17, 1994.

2. Peter Fryer, *Staying Power: The History of Black People in Britain* (London and Sydney: Pluto Press, 1974), 228; Douglas Lorimer, *Colour, Class and the Victorians: English Attitudes to the Negro in the Mid-Nineteenth Century* (Leicester and New York: Leicester University Press and Holmes & Meier, 1978), 212–13; Malcolm I. Thomis and Jennifer Grimmett, *Women in Protest 1800–1850* (New York: St. Martin's Press, 1982).

3. A. L. Morton, *A People's History of England* (New York: International Publishers, 1938), 387.

4. Eric J. Hobsbawm, *Industry and Empire,* Pelican Economic History of Britain, vol. 3 (London: Penguin Books, 1968), 89.

5. The thesis that slavery was abolished because it was becoming unprofitable has been intensely debated for decades. Its main proponents have been C. L. R. James, *The Black Jacobins: Toussaint L'Ouverture and the San Domingo Revolution* (London: Secker & Warburg, 1938), and Eric Williams, *Capitalism and Slavery* (New York: Capricorn Books, 1944), 132 and passim.

6. David Thomson, *England in the Nineteenth Century* (Baltimore, MD: Penguin, 1950), 16–17.

7. Fryer, *Staying Power,* 213.

8. *Hansard Parliamentary Debates,* Commons, 3d ser., vols. 1–3 (1830–31). Entry under "Slavery" in no. 11.

9. Information about Bermuda can be found in Henry C. Wilkinson, *Bermuda from Sail to Steam: The History of the Island from 1784–1901,* vols. 1 and 2 (London: Oxford University Press, 1973), and Walter Brownell Hayward, *Bermuda Past and Present: A Descriptive and Historical Account of the Somers Islands* (New York: Dodd, Mead and Co., 1911). For a full discussion of the status of slaves in Bermuda, see Cyril Outerbridge Packwood, *Chained on the Rock: Slavery in Bermuda* (New York: Eliseo Torres; Bermuda:

Baxter's Limited, 1975). Most of the details about Bermuda in the text come from these sources. Jean Kennedy, *Isle of Devils: Bermuda under the Somers Island Co. 1609–1685* (Hamilton, Bermuda: Collins in association with Baxter's, 1971) provides valuable information on early industrial development. With respect to Mary Prince's family, the parish records for Brackish Pond for both births and marriages do not begin until 1822 so very little is known outside of the text. I have checked the Devonshire Parish Assessment Books; Index of Slaves' Names; General Index of Manumissions and Bills of Sale of Slaves Contained in Books of Miscellanies; Early Bermuda Wills 1629–1835; and the Devonshire Parish Records for 1798–1839. See note 16. The Assessments of Warwick Parish do not survive. Regarding the "owners," Packwood gives data on the mercantilist (and profiteering) Triminghams (36, 39), while Wilkinson provides ample data about the Darrell family, including a note about the celebration of a birthday dinner for the king that Richard Darrell organized in 1809 after becoming "the new mayor of Hamilton" (vol. 1, 226). A Richard Darrell has eleven female slaves listed in the registry, and so the first name of Mary Prince's mother may be on that list. The Pruden family is mentioned in Wilkinson, vol. 1, 387. An old house in Murrell's Vale where Mary Prince lived with the Prudens is still standing and may have been their residence. I thank Sonia Grant for a fascinating visit to that house. The best overall source for white families is Clara Frances Edith Hollis Hallett, *Bermuda Index 1784–1914: An Index of Births, Marriages, Deaths, as Recorded in Bermuda Newspapers,* vol. 2 (Bermuda: Juniperhill Press, 1989). Vernon Jackson also drew my attention to the general area of Spanish Point where Mr. Jackson believes that Capt. John Ingham lived and grazed his cattle. The only pond in the Spanish Point (Pembroke West) area is the Pembroke Canal, which starts at Mills Creek near the bottom of Cox's Hill and runs in a generally easterly direction to Pembroke Marsh in Pembroke East. It is possible, concludes Mr. Jackson, that Capt. Ingham's farm and grazing land occupied a part of the low land below Cox's Hill, Sandy Hill, and/or Mount Hill,—somewhere in that area. A very old house still standing, he speculates, might possibly be Capt. Ingham's house. Note that the Darrell and Trimingham families have a variant spelling in Mary Prince's text.

10. Wilkinson, *Bermuda from Sail to Steam,* vol. 1, 23; Hayward, *Bermuda Past and Present,* 50. Packwood gives population statistics for 1774: there were 5,632 whites and 5,023 blacks. A tax was imposed on slave imports in the 1770s to limit their number, and in 1785 "a new tax on slaves and free Blacks became law" (Pack-

wood, *Chained on the Rock,* 79). It is impossible to tell from the text whether Mary Prince's parents were first generation slaves.

11. Packwood, *Chained on the Rock,* 3; Wilkinson, *Bermuda from Sail to Steam,* vol. 1, 28. The most important secondary source (quoting directly from the Manchester Papers) about the founding of Bermuda and the original black inhabitants is Wesley Frank Craven, "An Introduction to the History of Bermuda," parts 1–4, *William and Mary Quarterly* 17 (April 1937): 176–215; (July 1937): 317–62; (October 1937): 437–65; 18 (January 1938): 13–63. Information supplied about black settlers in Craven, "Introduction," part 2, 358–62 makes it clear that black men were experts and instructed the white colonists in their most important potential industries: pearl diving, the care of sugarcane and tropical and subtropical plants, and the growing and curing of tobacco. "Francisco, Antonye, and James" are three who are specifically mentioned (360–61). See note 31.

12. One rebellion, in November 1656, was led by a dozen black men, including men named Black Tom and Cabilecto. They intended to "distroie . . . the English in the night," but several slaves collaborated and Black Tom was hanged and Cabilecto executed on a gibbet. For details of the 1656 conspiracy, see Packwood, *Chained on the Rock,* 142, and Michael Craton, *Testing the Chains: Resistance to Slavery in the British West Indies* (Ithaca, N.Y.: Cornell University Press, 1982), 225–26. Another plot erupted seventeen years later at Christmas under the leadership of five slaves, one of whom turned (or more likely was tortured into turning) traitor. After these outbreaks, Governor John Heydon put strict laws into effect (Packwood, *Chained on the Rock,* 143–45). Mary Prince was most likely to have heard of plots devised by slaves that occurred within her parents' lifetimes. Between 1720 and 1730, several remarkable poisoning plots that involved slaves knowledgeable about plants and herbs were uncovered. After the poisoning of several whites, a very old slave named Sarah or Sally Bassett was burnt at the stake for being a ringleader and attained legendary status. The poisoning plots, including the central role of Sarah Bassett, are discussed in detail by Packwood (146–49). In 1761, an islandwide plot by over half the black population led to a law being enacted in 1762 that called for extensive vigilance over black people, especially at night. Such historical tales would have strengthened the already keen sense of self that Prince's environment guaranteed (Packwood, *Chained on the Rock,* 149–57). Since many whites thought free black people were responsible for these plots, regulations against them were tightened. "This was the last really big conspiracy, planned by Blacks,

during slavery. Well over half of Bermuda's slave population of approximately 4,000, were prepared to rebel against almost 5,000 white inhabitants" (Packwood, *Chained on the Rock,* 156). See also K. E. Ingram, comp. and ed., *Source for West Indian Studies: A Supplementary Listing, with Particular Reference to Manuscript Sources* (Switzerland: Inter Documentation Co Ag Zug, 1983). In item 0935, p. 261 (Letter to the Lords Commissioners of Trade and Plantations, February 28, 1762, British Library Shelfmark BB of.1.a.), William Popple (1701–64; Governor of Bermuda, 1745–64) gives "an account of an intended insurrection of Negroes and of the measures taken to suppress it."

13. The Bermuda Archives containing parish records and assessments indicate that the Trimingham, Darrell, Williams, and Pruden families were intimately connected through marriage. It is also possible that the Inghams, Darrells, and possibly the Woods were interconnected through marriage. See especially *Bermuda Index* listings under these family names. See, for example, the following entry:

> INGHAM, Joseph Wood, 1834 May 20.
> Son-in-law and exec. of will of Elizabeth Darrell White of Pembroke (widoe of John), wife Ann Wood (daugh. of John deceased, and Eliz. Darrell White), also executor. Children: MARGARET AMELIA PRINCE, Adelaide Horne. (*Bermuda Index,* C. F. E. Hollis Hallett, ed., 308)

Vernon Jackson of Hamilton Parish, Bermuda, informed me that Murrell's Vale where the Prudens lived still exists today in Paget Parish and is probably the place where Mary Prince went to work. I thank John Aden and Vernon Jackson for leading me to important sources. For an update on the Darrells, see H. A. Leseur, "Richard Darrell—Patriarch of Hamilton," *Royal Gazette Special Supplement,* August 29, 1959.

14. *History,* 47. For a discussion of the politics of childhood recollections, see Frances Smith Foster, *Witnessing Slavery: The Development of Ante-Bellum Slave Narratives* (Westport, CT, and London: Greenwood Press, 1979), 95–96 and passim. Foster argues that many slave narratives depict childhood as "a fairly happy time punctuated by incidents which temporarily disturbed the individual and foreshadowed for the reader the disasters to come" (96).

15. Minrose C. Gwin, "Green-Eyed Monsters of the Slavocracy: Jealous Mistresses in Two Slave Narratives," in *Conjuring: Black Women, Fiction, and Literary Tradition,* ed. Marjorie Pryse and Hortense J. Spillers (Bloomington: Indiana University Press, 1985),

42, 40. In the same volume, see also Frances Smith Foster, "Adding Color and Contour to Early American Self-Portraitures: Autobiographical Writings of Afro-American Women," 25–38. Foster discusses three forms of African American slave narratives: the spiritual (Jarena Lee), the travel (Nancy Prince), and autobiographical fiction (Harriet Wilson) (26–27). The limitations imposed by transcriber and audience affected slave narratives transatlantically. "The black woman was indeed measured by the standards of the nineteenth-century 'Cult of True Womanhood,' as Erlene Stetson suggests, but her situation of enslavement prevented her from being able to live up to the Victorian ideal of chastity" (Foster, "Adding Color and Contour," 42). Foster also discusses the issue of rape in "Adding Color and Contour" (31) and in *Witnessing Slavery* (108–9). If one adds to these difficulties the rigorous religious-evangelical dimension of the people Mary Prince dealt with in the Anti-Slavery Society and the fact that they played a major role in determining how her *History* was presented, it is easy to understand her probable recourse to coded strategies.

16. Under entries for both Daniel and Frances Trimingham the Devonshire Parish Assessments for 1663–1799 explicitly state the joint ownership of Prince. For an update on the Trimingham family, see Andrew Trimingham, "All the Way to Crow Lane Side: Nothing There but Foolish Pride. A Quick look at the Birth, Life and Death of Paget 'Society'," *Bermudian* (May 1991): 32–34, 101; see also "Generations in Business, Trimingham's—Established 1842," *Royal Gazette Special Supplement,* August 29, 1959.

17. This information comes from the Devonshire Parish Assessments.

18. In the supplement to Mary Prince's narrative, Thomas Pringle declined to print in full the names of Captain Ingham and his wife (and D——) because they were dead when the narrative was published and would have to "answer at a far more awful tribunal." Besides, Pringle added, "it might deeply lacerate the feelings of their surviving and perhaps innocent relatives" (preface, iii–iv). Evidence found in the Bermuda Archives, Hamilton, Bermuda, documents that Capt. and Mrs. I were John Ingham and Mary Spencer, who were married on September 26, 1789. The Inghams lived at Spanish Point, and they had a son named Benjamin who was baptized on October 16, 1790 (document supplied by the archivist, Bermuda Archives). Mary Prince states that the Inghams lived at Spanish Point and had a son, Benjy, who was roughly her own age. In the Slave Registry 1820–21 listing all slaves born in Bermuda, a *Captain* Ingham had only three slaves listed, none with names similar to those in the *History*. Further information regarding the Inghams

appears in C. F. E. Hollis Hallett's *Bermuda Index 1784–1914*. The *Bermuda Index* for September 26, 1789, states that Captain John Ingham married Miss Mary Spencer Albuoy, both of Spanish Point. No date is given. The *Index* also records the birth of a son, Benjamin, to John and Mary Ingham in Pembroke Parish, on October 16, 1790 (see also n. 9). Vernon Jackson, who has carefully researched the Ingham family, provided me with the following supplementary facts. He begins with information from Lefroy's *Memorials* (J. H. Lefroy, *Memorials of the Discovery and Early Settlement of the Bermudas or Somers Islands 1515–1685*. 2 vols [Bermuda Government Library, 1932].): "Probably the first Ingham to arrive in Bermuda was one John Ingham who in 1663 occupied a tenement and share of land (owned by John Darrell) in Pembroke Parish near the border with Devonshire. So that would be a few miles from the area where I believe Captain John Ingham had his house and farm,—and it was 125 years before Mary Prince was born."

I am further indebted to Vernon Jackson for the following commentary, in private correspondence to Moira Ferguson, that also pertains to Captain Ingham and his family.

As far as exact location is concerned, we know that Captain Ingham lived in a "large house built at the bottom of a very high hill at Spanish Point," and we are told that the cattle were staked out "about the pond side." The only pond in the Spanish Point (Pembroke West) area is the Pembroke Canal which starts at Mills Creek near the bottom of Cox's Hill and runs in a generally easterly direction to Pembroke Marsh in Pembroke East. We have to conclude therefore that Captain Ingham's farm and grazing land occupied a part of the low land below Cox's Hill, Sandy Hill and/or Mount Hill,—somewhere in that area.

The following story, Vernon Jackson continues, lends a little support to the preceding.

About two years ago I met a white Bermudian woman who for many years had resided in Canada. She was born in Bermuda, a member of the Ingham family. She told me that her family had operated a farm and dairy for many long years, even long before she was born, and she is now about my age, so that farm probably extended way back into the 1800's. Their home was near the Electric Light Station, and the farm and dairy animals grazed along the sides of the Pembroke Canal. She further explained that about 1924 she and her family moved from Pembroke to land they had bought in Smith's Parish. She said it was a Sunday morning when they drove all the cows and other farm animals along the public road from Pembroke West to Smith's Parish. What I am saying is that this Ingham family had a farm and dairy business approximately where Captain Ingham lived and had his farm. I could also add that up to about 1950, Harry King's dairy cows grazed on the same land, which is where Burland & Co., the Telephone Co. and Ray Brothers Garage are now located.

Finally, when I was a young boy, early every morning, I had to pedal out to the home of Joseph Ingham at Cox's Hill to get milk for my family. He was a farmer and a dairy-man. He was one of 3 brothers, Joseph, Austen and Charles Ingham. They were all married and lived within a stone's throw of each other. They were members of a coloured INGHAM family who have lived at Cox's Hill for more than 100 years. A patriach of this family, some-where back in the last century bought (or was bequeathed) a large tract of land at Cox's Hill which was called "Ingham Vale" and with great forethought he divided it among his children and grandchildren. So today the coloured Inghams are well en-trenched at Cox's Hill. One of them is today the Vice President of the Electric Light Co.

It is also worth noting Thomas Pringle's background in the light of his shielding of slave abusers. Thomas Pringle spent many years in South Africa after personal economic collapse in Scotland, gaining a small reputation as a poet. He typified the vast majority of aboli-tionists who were deeply committed to emancipation but more often than not held white supremacist attitudes toward Africans. This perspective is decidedly evident in Pringle's poetry. In *Staying Power,* Peter Fryer relates an anecdote that highlights these reali-ties: "When members and friends of the African and Asian Society dined at a tavern in 1816, with Wilberforce in the chair, the token Africans and Asians invited to the gathering were separated from the other guests by a screen set across one end of the room" (234). For further information on Thomas Pringle, see Thomas Pringle, *His Life, Times, and Poems* (Cape Town: J.C. Juta, 1912); and John Robert Doyle Jr., *Thomas Pringle* (New York: Twayne, 1972). There are other texts on Pringle that gloss over or do not present at all any information on his conventionally negative views of Afri-cans, such as the whitewashing introduction in Thomas Pringle, *Narrative of a Residence in South Africa. A New Edition. To which is prefixed a biographical sketch of the author by Josiah Condor* (London: Edward Moxon, 1840). I have found no text that explains the circumstances of Mary Prince and the outcome of the trials.

19. So far no record has been found of the burial of a Hetty who was the slave of Captain Ingham. That could mean she did not have an official burial due to her condition and Captain Ingham's fear of publicity. The impunity with which Mary Prince's owners abused their slaves is hardly surprising in view of the attitudes that allowed the treadwheel to be introduced on the island in the late 1820s as a "normal corrective expedient" and a substitute for whipping: "When a slave or a free man was sentenced to hard labour, this usually entailed a series of sessions on the treadwheel for stated periods of time" (James E. Smith, *Slavery in Bermuda* [New York: Vantage Press, 1938], 234). A woman named Lydia was sentenced to be worked on the treadwheel six times for stealing a doubloon: "She evidently suffered considerably from the exertion, and when taken off, could not, without assistance, retain an upright position" (Smith, *Slavery in Bermuda*, 235).

20. According to Addison Emery Verrill, *The Bermuda Islands* (New Haven, CT, 1907), an "earthquake is recorded Feb. 19, 1801" (510). The *Bermuda Royal Gazette,* November 22nd, 1831 also records the following:

> On Thursday morning, the 19th., [1801] about ten minutes after 9 o'clock, a violent earthquake was felt in St. George's; it came with a rumbling noise similar to thunder and lasted several seconds; it shook the homes very much and was very visibly felt in vessels and boats in the water. Its direction appeared as coming from the NW. It was also felt very heavily throughout these Islands.

> Terry Tucker, *Beware the Hurricane! The Story of the Gyratory Tropical Storms That Have Struck Bermuda and the Islanders' Folk-Lore Regarding Them* (Bermuda Historical Society, Occasional Publication no. 8), mentions a report from the *Bermuda Gazette* of October 26, 1793, that states that a hurricane blew "with the most violent rage all the morning; from eight to eleven it was at its height . . . and caused the greatest destruction" (71). By coincidence during this storm the brig *Adventure,* owned by Ingham, was "demasted, after driving with her anchors at her bows in the Great Sound" (Tucker, *Beware the Hurricane,* 72). This date is too early for Mary Prince, but Bermudian meteorologic conditions authenticate the account she gives.

21. Packwood, *Chained on the Rock,* 62. Packwood also notes that many slaves were transported as well as sold "throughout Bermuda's history," especially after plots were uncovered.
22. Wilkinson, *Bermuda from Sail to Steam,* vol. 1, 35.
23. In 1800, fifty-seven pounds Bermudian currency was thirty-eight pounds sterling. See *History,* 53, note *. See also Packwood, *Chained on the Rock,* 62, for exchange rates and currency information.
24. Despite an intensive search in the Bermudian Archives for likely entrepreneurs in the salt pond industry, property owners, and the like, the identity of D—— remains unknown. Of possible references to Mary Prince in the Slave Registry 1820–21, the one that appears on p. 76 seems the most likely: "Owner: Joseph Dill. Slave: Molly, female black houseservant age 28."
25. Erlene Stetson discusses female slave narratives in detail in "Studying Slavery: Some Literary and Pedagogical Considerations on the Black Female Slave," in *All the Women Are White, All the Blacks Are Men, but Some of Us Are Brave: Black Women's Studies,* ed. Gloria T. Hull, Patricia Bell Scott, and Barbara Smith (New York: Feminist Press, 1982).
26. Elsa V. Goveia, *Slave Society in the British Leeward Islands at the End of the Eighteenth Century* (New Haven, CT: Yale University Press, 1965), 238–40.
27. San Domingo's policy, established after the successful revolution in 1791, of receiving and protecting slaves on the run from Turks Island and elsewhere meant that escape and revolution (with a built-in possibility of success) were common subjects of discussion on Turks Island. See Packwood, *Chained on the Rock,* 47.
28. Mary Prince's intimations about abusive sexual involvement with D—— could be applied to her former situation at the home of Captain and Mrs. Ingham. The phenomenon of the jealous white wife—as Minrose Gwin argues—crops up in many slave narratives. Although Mary Prince scarcely hints at such activities, it is very likely that Captain Ingham might have taken advantage of an attractive and unprotected slave. This would partly explain why Mrs. Ingham acted so inhumanely:

> The next morning my mistress set about instructing me in my tasks. She taught me to do all sorts of household work; to wash and bake, pick cotton and wool, and wash floors, and cook. And she taught me (how can I ever forget it!) more things than these; she caused me to know the exact difference between the smart of

the rope, the cart-whip, and the cow-skin, when applied to my naked body by her own cruel hand. And there was scarcely any punishment more dreadful than the blows I received on my face and head from her hard heavy fist. She was a fearful woman, and a savage mistress to her slaves.

It is notable that Mary Prince's sexual life is extensively discussed by her enemies and her advocates in the apparatus surrounding her text. For further discussion see Moira Ferguson, *Subject to Others: British Women Writers and Colonial Slavery 1678–1834* (New York: Routledge, 1992) 281–98; and in the court cases attached herein as appendix 5 and 6. Clearly Thomas Pringle et al. thought that such a sensitive and "distasteful" subject should be interrogated only by men.

29. The transcriber of Mary Prince's manuscript was Susanna Strickland, who also wrote *Enthusiasm; and Other Poems* (London: Smith, Elder, & Co., 1831) and was a recently converted Methodist. The volume was dedicated to the Moravian editor James Montgomery, an abolitionist. One of the poems in that volume is entitled "An Appeal to the Free." She was the sister of Eliza and Agnes Strickland, the latter of whom wrote the celebrated *Lives of the Queens of England.* 12 vols. (London: Henry Colburn, 1840), 48. Susanna Strickland married Major John Dunbar Moodie at St. Pancras Church, 1831, emigrated to Canada, and continued to write. Initial evidence that the transcriber was Susanna Strickland Moodie appears in the appendix to Tract 1512, no. 5, British Library Shelfmark T1512(5) (see appendix 3 of this volume). Mary Pringle, Thomas Pringle's wife, who informs Lucy Townsend of the Birmingham Ladies' Society for Relief of Negro Slaves that several women witnessed the scars on Mary Prince's body, states that one of the witnesses was "Miss Strickland (the lady who wrote down in this house the narratives of Mary Prince and Ashton Warner)." Sara Eaton, *Lady of Backwoods: A Biography of Catherine Parr Traill* (Toronto, Montreal: McClelland & Stewart, 1969), mentions that Thomas Pringle gave the bride away when Susanna Strickland married John Moodie. Susanna Strickland had been received into the Methodist community at Bungay, Suffolk, shortly before. A similarity in their religious beliefs probably attracted both Pringle and Strickland to Mary Prince's narrative. Further biographical information is available in Susanna Moodie, *Roughing It in the Bush or Life in Canada*, ed. Carl Ballstadt (Ottawa: Carleton University Press, 1988), xvii–xviii, lii–liv; and in Una Constance Birch,

afterward Pope-Hennessy, *Agnes Strickland, Biographies of the Queens of England, 1796–1874* (London: Chatto & Windus, 1940). For further information, see note 52.

30. Vernon Jackson provides the following history of Cedar Hills, and from it, comments Jackson, "I conclude that John Till was probably Mary Prince's master while she worked there. (Till occupied the property from 1813 to 1822.)"

On August 22nd, 1803, six lots of land known collectively as "Cedar Hills" and "Underwood" at Ferry Reach, St. George's West, were granted by King George III to Joseph Hutchinson, Esq. of England. There was no tax on the land, so it remained in its pristine state, undisturbed and undeveloped.

In 1806 John Till and his wife Maria arrived in Bermuda from England. In a recent article I described him as a "colourful character." He had sailed to the East Indies as a purser, but after arrival in St. George's he was classified as a "shopman" in Gosling's store. He was said to be an energetic and helpful fellow who soon progressed in the commercial life of St. George's.

He acquired two prize vessels which he sold at a fair profit; and as a result, on August 21st, 1813 he was able to purchase the Cedar Hills and Underwood property from Hutchinson, with John Adkins holding a substantial mortgage. Till built a house. He had some dairy cattle and a few slaves, and before long there were little Johnnies and Marias running around Cedar Hills.

John Till was a purveyor of goods to the army and navy, and for a brief period he was a junior partner of Ambrose Gosling who was the first one to employ him in St. George's.

On a trip to England in 1814, Till was commissioned to buy a clock for the square tower in St. Peter's Church. He found one in Portsmouth, and it was eventually installed in a raised and enlarged tower at St. Peter's.

John Till began to prosper. He was a good churchman and a good family man. Ambrose Gosling was godfather for one of his children. Till sat on the magistrates' bench, and after he distinguished himself by horse-whipping the unpopular Colonial Secretary Robert Kennedy, the St. Georgians elected him as their Mayor to reward him for his "valor." He even served an unimpressive short term in the House of Assembly.

His Nemesis was the Governor himself, Sir William Lumley, who made life so difficult for Till that he fell behind in his mortgage payments to John Adkins. Therefore, by a natural sequence of events, the next step in this chronicle occurred when John

Adkins (by a decree of the Supreme Court) took possession of the property on March 22, 1822.

This meant that John Till no longer had the right of access to the Cedar Hills property. From then on it was all downhill. He slowly but surely lost his grip. He was reduced to running the St. George's Coney Island ferry, but drunkenness soon made that impossible. Finally on May 26th, 1829, he was found drowned at Ferry Reach, the inquest deciding that he died "while in a state of delirium." His wife lived on to the good age of 89. Their nine children all married, except for those who died early in life.

But this story is about the land rather than about the people who lived on it, so lets [*sic*] return to John Adkins and see what happened after he took possession: he kept the land until he felt it was time for a change; then, by his will of July 27th, 1837, he devised that land to his only son, John Petty-Adkins.

Now the young man was not interested in keeping the land, but he was interested in turning it into cash that he badly needed. So he advertised the sale by auction, with the result that on May 19th, 1846 a crowd gathered for the sale, and the highest bidder took possession after paying only £604 for those many acres of good land.

And who was this man who could put his hand on £604 cash in the year 1846? Believe it or not, he was a coloured man, a successful mason/farmer named Robert James Packwood who had left Smith's parish and settled at the East End, and who, only 12 years after Emancipation, surprised St. Georgians when he became the new owner of the Cedar Hills and Underwood Property.

That, by the way, is not the climax of this story. Robert James Packwood never got around to making a will, so when he died intestate in 1866, his older son Dr. Richard Arnold Packwood, became the heir, and other members of that family began to wistfully picture themselves owning some of the land.

But Dr. Packwood had a dream that went far beyond his family. His dream included the children of the future. In 1924 he willed "the farm lands, woods and buildings named Cedar Hills and Underwood at Ferry Reach", in trust to the Berkeley Institute for the furtherance of higher education of children in Bermuda.

That land was prime real estate. It was very valuable. After much negotiating, it was sold for around £42,000 to the American millionaire John Jacob Astor who built a luxury home there overlooking the waters of Ferry Reach. That £42,000 was probably the equivalent of one million dollars in today's currency.

How very providential that was! In 1924 when other schools

of higher learning were equipped with classrooms, science labs, assembly halls, gyms and playing fields—Berkeley had two class rooms and very little else.

So picture the elation this windfall caused. Immediately the Berkeley governors started planning for the future. Bankers, lawyers, architects and builders were consulted, and the result, covering a period of some years, is what you see there today.

Dr. Packwood's philanthropy did not stop there. Before he died, he arranged for the property in Somerset known as the Packwood Home to be used in perpetuity as a retirement home for the elderly.

People who knew Dr. Packwood as a medical practitioner more than 70 years ago, might have forgotten what he looked like, but we can never forget his great foresight. The monuments are there for us to see and enjoy.

The long chain of events that caused the Ferry Reach property to change hands, finally and unerringly led to great and inexpressible benefits for many people, past, present and yet unborn. (V. Jackson, *Paradise Found—Almost* [Bermuda: Globe Press, 1996], 220–22)

I thank Vernon Jackson most warmly for this helpful information, for fruitful discussions regarding other issues discussed in the text, and for valuable documentation.

31. For information about Antiguan law, see Mrs. Flanders, *Antigua and the Antiguans: A Full Account of the Colony and its Inhabitants From the Time of the Caribs to the Present Day, Interspersed with Anecdotes and Legends. Also, an Impartial View of Slavery and the Free Labour Systems; The Statistics of the Island, and Biographical Notices of the Principal Families*, vols. 1 and 2 (London: Saunders & Otley, 1844), 155–63. See also Vere Langford Oliver, *The History of the Island of Antigua, One of the Leeward Caribbees in the West Indies. From the First Settlement in 1635 to the Present Time* (London: Mitchell and Hughes, 1896); and Bryan Edwards, *The History, Civil and Commercial of the British Colonies in the West Indies*, vol. 2, quoted in Goveia, *Slave Society*, 218ff. and 315 and passim. It is possible that the prevalence of free blacks in Antigua spurred Mary Prince to deeper levels of resistance. Antigua was also the island that boasted two stalwart heroes of slave uprisings, Tacky and Tomboy. See Craton, *Testing the Chains*, 115–24, and David Barry Caspar, "The Antiguan Slave Conspiracy of 1736: A Case Study of the Origins of Collective

Resistance," *William and Mary Quarterly* 35 (April 1978): 308–23. For a thorough discussion of black Bermudians in preabolition days, including their work as skilled artisans and artists and as resistance fighters, see Kenneth E. Robinson, *Heritage* . . . (Hamilton, Bermuda: Macmillan and Berkeley Educational Society, 1979), 1–171. The ease with which so many British accepted slavery is evident in the texts of visitors to the island. Take Maria Riddell, *Voyages to the Madeira and Leeward Caribbean Isles: With Sketches of the Natural History of These Islands* (Edinburgh: Peter Hill; London: T. Cadell, 1792), 47–104, for example. In this narrative about her visit, Riddell confines her comments about the island's black inhabitants to their breeding of goats, selling of fur, catching of lizards, eating of prickly pears and cassava, use of calabashes, and making cradles from cabbage trees.

32. This question of the power accruing from taking a white lover is integral to Harriet Jacobs [Linda Brent], *Incidents in the Life of a Slave Girl* (San Diego, New York, London: Harcourt Brace Jovanovich, 1973). For a discussion of the treatment of interracial sexual relationships in Antigua, see Packwood, *Chained on the Rock*, 82–87. In *Sex and Race: A History of White, Negro, and Indian Miscegenation on the Two Americas* (New York: J. A. Rogers, n.d.), J. A. Rogers argues that white men preferred black women sexually, and "in the face of this rivalry . . . married ladies frequently excelled their husbands in the use of the whip . . . Delicate young ladies had Negroes, male and female, stripped and beaten before them . . . Starved for love, they saw sex, whirling in abundance before them" (2, 130).

33. A white cooper, Peter Burchell, from a well-known slave-owning family, is mentioned as owning thirty-nine slaves in 1830 (Packwood, *Chained on the Rock*, 69; *A History of Mary Prince*, 71). He was one of Prince's prospective purchasers (See Mary Prince's testimony in *Wood v. Pringle*, 129). Documentation about Adam White, a "free black" according to Mary Prince's testimony, 81, can be found in Vere Langford Oliver, *The History of the Island of Antigua*, vol. 10 (1896). Adam White signed "The Petition of the Coloured Inhabitants of the Island of Antigua" addressed to the House of Commons on April 17, 1830, expressing concern about the "political disabilities" of free blacks (Oliver, *History of the Island*, clii). Further information on Capt. Abbott as a lover of Mary Prince appears in the court report of *Wood v. Pringle*, 130–32.

34. G. W. F. Hegel, *Phenomenology of Spirit*, trans. A. V. Miller (Oxford: Clarendon Press, 1977), 111–19.

35. For an analysis of Hegel that foregrounds Hegel's master/slave

discussion, see Alexandre Kojève, *Introduction to the Reading of Hegel. Lectures on the Phenomenology of Spirit Assembled by Raymond Queneau,* ed. Allen Bloom and trans. James H. Nichols (New York: Basic Books, 1969), esp. 3–31.

36. The bill for the emancipation of slaves was introduced into Parliament in 1823 and passed ten years later. Information about British women's antislavery agitation can be found in Moira Ferguson, *Subject to Others: British Writers and Colonial Slavery, 1678–1834* (New York: Routledge, 1992). There were several contemporary antislavery publications, most notably the *Anti-Slavery Reporter,* as well as *The Tourist: A Literary and Anti-Slavery Journal. Under the Superintendance of the Agency Anti-Slavery Society,* British Library Shelfmark PP5295.

37. Angela Davis, "Reflections on the Black Women's Role in the Community of Slaves," *Black Scholar* (December 1971): 3–15; Craton, *Testing the Chains,* 17. Beyond that, Mary Prince left a legacy behind that continued into the twentieth century. See, for example, Meredith Ebbin, "Gladys Misick Morrell and the Women's Suffrage Movement," *Bermudian* (May 1991): 66–69.

38. The British Museum copy of the *History* carries the following handwritten dedication on the title page: "The Reverend Mr Mortimer. With the Editor's best respects," British Library Shelfmark 8154bbb30. The Reverend Mortimer may be the individual mentioned in the *Dictionary of National Biography,* ed. Sir Leslie Stephen and Sir Sidney Lee (Oxford: Oxford University Press, 1917) who in 1833 wrote *The Immediate Abolition of Slavery compatible with the safety and prosperity of the colonies,* British Library Shelfmark 8156aaa67.

39. Joseph Phillips was already a noted opponent of the proslavery lobby and had been embroiled in altercations with the notorious James Macqueen, editor of the *Glasgow Courier,* over the relief of distressed slaves in Antigua. Phillips is mentioned in *Oliver, History of the Island,* vol. 10, cli, in connection with the free blacks' petition (see note 31).

> The necessary explanations and information accompany the Petition, which will be handed you by Mr. Joseph Phillips, a native of England, to whom I beg to refer you for any information which may be required. He is intimately acquainted from his long residence in this Island with every particular connected with the West India system, and has himself been much persecuted and oppressed, having married a lady of colour by whom he has several children.

Phillips later wrote *West Indian Question: The Outline of a Plan for the Total, Immediate, and Safe Abolition of Slavery Throughout the British Colonies* (London: J. & A. Arch, 1833). Macqueen went on to attack Thomas Pringle and Mary Prince in an article in the well-known periodical, *Blackwood's Magazine* (November 1831), which was entitled "The Colonial Empire of Great Britain. Letter to Earl Grey, First Lord of the Treasury, etc., etc., for James Macqueen esq.," 744–64. Thomas Pringle sued the publisher of *Blackwood's Magazine,* Thomas Cadell, at the Court of Common Appeals on February 22, 1832, and won. On February 27, 1833, on behalf of the West Indian Lobby, John Wood sued Thomas Pringle. Wood won by default. For information on Capt. Abbott, see note 33.

40. Goveia, *Slave Society,* 285. For more information on Antiguan Moravians, see also Flanders, *Antigua and the Antiguans,* 234–52.
41. Goveia, *Slave Society,* 269.
42. See Packwood, *Chained on the Rock,* 77–84, 120–21, 154–55 and passim, for a discussion of free blacks and the persistent controversy over granting them manumission.
43. See appendix 1, "Mary Prince's Petition," which indicates how much Mary Prince restrained herself in offering reasons for leaving the Woods' household. According to Thomas Pringle, John Wood represented Prince to her advocates as an "abandoned and worthless woman, ungrateful towards him, and undeserving of sympathy from others." He produces "evidence" from proslavery friends to corroborate his allegations. His maneuver was successful in that the abolitionist Stephen Lushington, deeming it in Mary Prince's best interests not to have the matter debated in Parliament, "Abstain[ed] from any remarks on [Wood's] conduct when the petition was at last presented in Parliament. In this way [Wood] dexterously contrived to neutralize all our efforts, until the close of the session of 1829; soon after which he embarked with his family for the West Indies" (26).

    Lushington is concerned about the aspersions cast by the Woods about Prince's "immorality." Joseph Phillips's statements on that subject are very telling for he reminds readers that Wood's allegations about Mary Prince's "immorality" would be evaluated negatively only in Britain. Such "immoral conduct" in the West Indies—relationships between white men and black women—is "so common, I might almost say universal" that this would not be considered immoral. As if to stress the moral status of his family, Wood's daughter Mary, a witness in the trial of Wood versus Pringle was married in 1832 in Antigua. Oddly enough, the minister who marries her bears the same name as the male slave Ashton Warner, whose narrative was transcribed by Susanna Strickland.

> 1832, May 29: Mary Caroline Wood, eldest daughter of John A. Wood, married John Bennet, eldest son of John Bennet, in Antigua on April 25, at St. George's Church, Fitches Creek, by Rev. Ashton Warner. (*Antigua Herald,* April 28, recorded in *Bermuda Index,* 1784–1914, ed. C. F. E. Hollis Hallett, 1548)

Invoking a double standard, Wood is striving "for effect in England" (32). Note also that in 1836, John Adams Wood, "aged 53, a native of Bermuda, and a merchant of Antigua, died in London on Jan. 29, after an illness of two days." C. F. E. Hollis Hallett, *Bermuda Index,* vol. 2, 1548.

44. Even in this century, the conduct of the Woods is still being vindicated. In William Zuill, *Bermuda Sampler 1815–1850 Being a Collection of Newspaper Items, Extracts from Books and Private Papers, together with many Explanatory Notes and a Variety of Illustrations* (1937; reprint, Bungay, Suffolk: Richard Clay & Son, n.d.), for example, appears the following section. It should be noted that Zuill was a white native Bermudian, reprinting a nineteenth-century vilification:

> *Mischievous interference of the Anti-Slavery Society. Mr. Wood,* a highly respectable merchant of Antigua, many years ago, in Bermuda, purchased for 67 pounds sterling, a slave named *Mary Prince* who earnestly entreated him to buy her and relieve her from the miserable situation in which she states herself to have been. After living in *Mr. Wood's* family for 13 years, during which time he paid her ten guineas a year, on *Mr. Wood* preparing to come to England, she begged so hard to go with him and her mistress, *Mr. Wood* was induced to permit her, on her earnest entreaty that change of climate would benefit her health, and as an encouragement to good behaviour, promised that she should be set free on her return to Antigua. In England her conduct became unbearable; she refused to work—declared that the roast beef and veal was "horseflesh"—that "she would not eat cold meat, not being accustomed to it in Antigua"; and after a variety of similar conduct was told by her master that she must either return to Antigua, or as she was free in England, she must leave his house, as he could not have the peace of his family disturbed by her. She at length left his house, taking with her

several trunks of clothes and about 40 guineas in money, which she had saved in *Mr. Wood's* service. The Anti-Slavery Society lent a not unwilling ear to the statement of this woman, and the result is the pamphlet before us, published under the editorship of the vilest description . . . We cannot omit stating that *Mr.* and *Mrs. Wood* who are thus calumniated by the hired advocate of the Anti-Slavery Society (who sees nothing but purity in a prostitute because she knew when to utter the name of the Deity, to turn up the whites of her eyes, and make a perfect mockery of religion), are described by the most respectable magistrates and members of council in Antigua as standing as high as human beings can stand. We take our leave of this disgusting conduct, which goes far to compromise a society, which numbers many eminent and worthy individuals among its members, by warning the public to receive with doubt and distrust, statements from a quarter so jaundiced on a great public question, which equally concerns the welfare of masters and slaves.—November 22nd, 1831. (144).

A long version of this extract (possibly the original from which Zuill drew his material) appears in an article entitled "The Anti-Slavery Society, and the West Indian Colonists" in the *Bermuda Royal Gazette* of November 22, 1831.

45. Packwood, *Chained on the Rock,* 63.
46. Foster, *Witnessing Slavery,* 55.
47. Foster, *Witnessing Slavery,* 44–46.
48. Stephen Butterfield, *Black Autobiography in America* (Amherst: University of Massachusetts Press, 1974), 16.
49. See *Letters of the Late Ignatius Sancho, an African* (London, 1782), i–ix. Joseph Jekyll prefixed to the letters a memoir of Sancho's early life. See also Folaris Shyllon, *Black People in Britain 1555–1833* (London, New York, Ibadan: Oxford University Press for the Institute of Race Relations, 1977), 187–95.
50. Documentation on Kitty Hylton, Kate, and Grace Jones is available in the *Anti-Slavery Reporter* 3, no. 66 (for Hylton); 2, no 47 (for Kate). For a thorough examination of the case of Grace Jones, see Folaris Shyllon, *Black Slaves in Britain* (London: Oxford University Press, 1974), 210–29. There are innumerable cases, other than those cited in the preceding, that involve abuses against female slaves. See, for example, the *Anti-Slavery Reporter* 4, no. 12. All of these cases occurred just before Mary Prince left Antigua or when she lived in London.
51. Philip D. Curtin, ed., *Africa Remembered: Narratives by West*

Africans from the Era of the Slave Trade (Madison: University of Wisconsin Press, 1967), 5.

52. Susanna Moodie, *Letters of a Lifetime,* ed. Carl Ballstadt, Elizabeth Hopkins, and Michael Peterman (Toronto: University of Toronto Press, 1985), 57. See also *Letters of Love and Duty: The Correspondence of Susanna and John Moodie,* ed. Carl Ballstadt, Elizabeth Hopkins, and Michael Peterman (Toronto: University of Toronto Press, 1993), 7 and passim.

53. Susanna Moodie, *Letters of a Lifetime,* 60.

54. Testimony by the Reverend James Curtin to the Committee of the House of Lords is reported in full in the *Anti-Slavery Reporter* (February 1833): 500–517. Curtin ventured that planters were "latterly" very loath to punish slaves because they "had a great deal of feeling for them" (501).

55. Evidence that slaves were abandoned was overwhelming. Macqueen's insistence that the slaves were lying was a standard ploy in proslavery propaganda. See for example the *West Indian Reporter* for 1830–31 and its ravings about the "designs" and "systematic slanders" of the "Anti-Colonial [antislavery] Party." The emancipationists on the other hand, and the *Anti-Slavery Reporter* in particular, took special care to check every fact because of the zeal of the proslavery lobby in trying to "expose" distortions. See "The Case of the Neglected and Deserted Negroes in the Island of Antigua," which details the ready abandonment by their owners of slaves who are sick or too old to be industrious (John Rylands University Library of Manchester, Anti-Slavery Collection, part 8 of box 21, item 5).

56. See *Reports of Cases Determined at Nisi Prius, in the Courts of King's Bench, Common Pleas, and Exchequer, and on the Northern and Western Circuits, from the Sittings after Michaelmas Term, 1 Will, IV. 1830, Sittings after Trinity Term, 7 Will. IV. 1836, Inclusive,* ed. William Moody and Frederic Robinson, vol. 1 (London: Saunders & Benning; J. and W. T. Clarke, 1837), 277; and *The English Reports,* vol. 174, *Nisi Prius 5* (London: W. Green; Edinburgh: Stevens & Sons, 1929), 95. For the earlier case in which Pringle sued Cadell, see the *Times* (London), February 22, 1833, p. 4, col. B. Since June Tomlinson and I could find no court records for this case despite an extensive search, we concluded that it was probably an unreported case. Pringle's biographers tend to gloss over the fact that he was involved in lawsuits just before he died. Some of the critics and biographers—John Robert Doyle Jr., is one—even gloss over Pringle's work for the Anti-Slavery Society and say nothing of Mary Prince. (Pringle lived in South Africa and wrote against slavery

there, prior to his becoming secretary for the Anti-Slavery Society. But he is filled with conventional contradictions. See note 18.) Pringle's friend, the Methodist Josiah Conder, who also wrote a biographical sketch, jumps chronologically from Pringle's acceptance of the Anti-Slavery Society's position in 1827 to his death in 1834. See Thomas Pringle, *Narrative of a Residence in South Africa. A New Edition. To Which is Prefixed a Biographical Sketch of the Author by Josiah Conder* (London: Edward Moxon, 1840). Pringle also wrote "The Slave-Dealer" in the Sheffield *Iris* newspaper for 1830 and helpfully corresponded with Mary Anne Rawson and contributed to her antislavery anthology, *The Bow in the Cloud* (London: Jackson and Walford, 1834). Pringle successfully suggested to Rawson that she include a poem by a West Indian free black man named Richard Hill. Pringle's involvement in court cases and the aspersions cast about Mary Prince's "immorality" and about Pringle's own conduct were probably subjects of deep embarrassment to the evangelical-Methodist emancipationists. Pringle's friend Leigh Ritchie reveals how these incidents affected Pringle and how Pringle intended to refute the allegations. His failing health and death made refutation impossible: "At the end of that time [receiving her into his house] he published her history as an anti-slavery tract; which gave rise in *Blackwood's Magazine* to a 'Criticism.' . . . He [Pringle] prosecuted the publisher, and obtained a verdict; but an action was brought against him by the West Indies body in the name of Wood; and owing to the difficulty and expense of obtaining legal evidence from the West Indies, he partly failed in proving the truth of his narrative and was cast in damages. Let me," continues editor Leigh Ritchie, "add this extract from one of his letters, dated 12 January 1832. 'The prosecution of Blackwood is not an affair of mine. I wished to have replied in print, and I will still do so in a fourth edition of the tract. The blackguardism I cannot reply to but there are some misrepresentations that require to be set right' " (*The Poetical Works of Thomas Pringle. With a Sketch of his life by Leigh Ritchie* [London: Edward Moson, 1838], 104–5).

57. Craton, *Testing the Chains,* 16.
58. *Times* (London), February 22, 1833, p. 4, col. B.
59. See note 56. See also Joan Grant, "Call Lord: The History of Mary Prince," *Trouble and Strife* 14 (autumn 1988): 9–12. L. Mathurin, *The Rebel Woman in the British West Indies during Slavery* (Kingston: Institute of Jamaica for the African-Caribbean Institute of Jamaica, 1975).
60. A search of Thomas Pringle's writings, his obituaries, correspondence between him and friends, biographical works, and related

material has so far failed to turn up any further information on Mary Prince. *The Athenaeum Journal of Literature, Science, and the Fine Arts,* the *Edinburgh Literary Journal or Weekly Register of Criticism and Belles Lettres,* and the *Monthly Review* yield no information on Mary Prince for the years 1831 to 1834 inclusive. Part of the difficulty might be that she was known—as the parliamentary petition indicates—by a number of names: Mary Prince, Mary Princess, Molly Wood, and Mary James. Moreover, until recently, not a great deal of information on writing by black women, either British or North American, was readily available. Among recent publications are Henry Louis Gates Jr., introduction to *Our Nig; or Sketches from the Life of a Free Black,* by Harriet E. Wilson (London: Allison & Busby, 1984). This introduction contains extensive biographical data about Wilson, who was the first black female novelist in the United States. Harriet Jacobs, *Incidents in the Life of a Slave Girl,* is another example (see note 32). The reissue of an early autobiography, *Wonderful Adventures of Mrs Seacole in Many Lands,* ed. Ziggi Alexander and Audrey Dewjee (1957; reprint, Bristol: Falling Wall Press, 1984), is the first work by a black British woman to appear in recent times. See also Erlene Stetson, "Studying Slavery" (n. 25). Stetson's text includes an extensive bibliography and considers the questions of the authenticity of slave narratives and the particular absence of extensive research on female slaves. A rich collection of many documents by and about black female slaves in North America can be found in Gerda Lerner, ed., *Black Women in White America: A Documentary History* (New York: Vintage Books, 1973). For further discussion, particularly of African American slave writings and philosophical and methodological approaches, see the following: William H. Robinson, *Phillis Wheatley and Her Writings* (New York and London: Garland, 1984); William L. Andrews, *To Tell a Free Story: The First Century of Afro-American Autobiography, 1760–1865* (Urbana and Chicago: University of Illinois Press, 1986); Dexter Fisher and Robert B. Stepto, eds., *Afro-American Literature: The Reconstruction of Instruction* (New York: Modern Language Association, 1979), especially three articles on Frederick D. Douglass's *Narrative* (1845) by Robert B. Stepto, Robert G. O'Meally, and Henry Louis Gates Jr. See also Sandra Pouchet Paquet, "The Heartbeat of a West Indian Slave: *The History of Mary Prince,*" *African American Review* 26 (spring 1992): 131–46; Barbara Bush, "Defiance or Submission? The Role of the Slave Woman in Slave Resistance in the British Caribbean," *Immigrants and Minorities* 1, (March 1982), 16–38; Barbara Bush, "White 'Ladies', Coloured

'Favourites' and Black 'Wenches': Some Considerations on Sex, Race and Class Factors in Social Relations in the British Caribbean," in *Slavery and Abolition: A Journal of Comparative Studies,* 2, no. 3: 245–62; Barbara Bush, "'The Family Tree Is Not Cut': Women and Cultural Resistance in Slave Family Life in the British Caribbean," in *In Resistance: Studies in African, Caribbean and Afro-American History,* ed. Gary Y. Okihiro (Amherst: University of Massachusetts Press, 1986).

———

THE HISTORY OF
MARY PRINCE

A West Indian Slave

Related by Herself

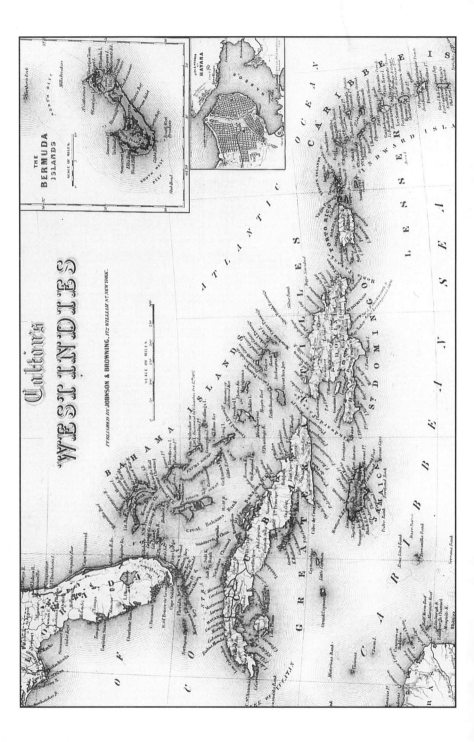

Colton's
WEST INDIES

PUBLISHED BY JOHNSON & BROWNING, 172 WILLIAM ST. NEW YORK.

SCALE OF MILES.

THE
BERMUDA
ISLANDS

SCALE OF MILES.

PLAN OF THE CITY & HARBOR OF
HAVANA

ATLANTIC   OCEAN

CARIBBEE   IS

WINDWARD ISLA

LESSER

ANTILLES

SEA

BAHAMA ISLANDS

Great Bahama Bank

CUBA

ST DOMINGO

PORTO RICO

JAMAICA

CARIBBEAN   SEA

GREAT   CARIBBEAN   SEA

GULF   OF   MEXICO

FLORIDA

Preface

The idea of writing Mary Prince's history was first suggested by herself. She wished it to be done, she said, that good people in England might hear from a slave what a slave had felt and suffered; and a letter of her late master's, which will be found in the Supplement, induced me to accede to her wish without farther delay. The more immediate object of the publication will afterwards appear.

The narrative was taken down from Mary's own lips by a lady who happened to be at the time residing in my family as a visitor. It was written out fully, with all the narrator's repetitions and prolixities, and afterwards pruned into its present shape; retaining, as far as was practicable, Mary's exact expressions and peculiar phraseology. No fact of importance has been omitted, and not a single circumstance or sentiment has been added. It is essentially her own, without any material alteration farther than was requisite to exclude redundances and gross grammatical errors, so as to render it clearly intelligible.

After it had been thus written out, I went over the whole, carefully examining her on every fact and circumstance detailed; and in all that relates to her residence in Antigua I had the advantage of being assisted in this scrutiny by Mr. Joseph Phillips, who was a resident in that colony during the same period, and had known her there.

The names of all the persons mentioned by the narrator have been printed in full, except those of Capt. I— and his wife, and that of Mr. D—, to whom conduct of peculiar atrocity is ascribed. These three individuals are now gone to answer at a far more awful tribunal than that of public opinion, for the deeds of which their former bondwoman accuses them; and to hold them up more openly to human reprobation could no longer affect themselves, while it might deeply lacerate the feelings of their surviving and perhaps innocent relatives, without any commensurate public advantage.

Without detaining the reader with remarks on other points which will be adverted to more conveniently in the Supplement, I shall here merely notice farther, that the Anti-Slavery Society have no concern whatever with this publication, nor are they in any degree responsible for the statements it contains. I have published the tract, not as their Secretary, but in my private capacity; and any profits that may arise from the sale will be exclusively appropriated to the benefit of Mary Prince herself.

THOMAS PRINGLE
7, Solly Terrace, Claremont Square,
January 25, 1831

P.S. Since writing the above, I have been furnished by my friend Mr. George Stephen, with the interesting narrative of Asa-Asa, a captured African, now under his protection; and have printed it as a suitable appendix to this little history.

T.P.

The History of Mary Prince
A West Indian Slave
Related by Herself

I was born at Brackish-Pond, in Bermuda, on a farm belonging to Mr. Charles Myners. My mother was a household slave; and my father, whose name was Prince, was a sawyer belonging to Mr. Trimmingham, a ship-builder at Crow-Lane. When I was an infant, old Mr. Myners died, and there was a division of the slaves and other property among the family. I was bought along with my mother by old Captain Darrel, and given to his grandchild, little Miss Betsey Williams. Captain Williams, Mr. Darrel's son-in-law, was master of a vessel which traded to several places in America and the West Indies, and he was seldom at home long together.

Mrs. Williams was a kind-hearted good woman, and she treated all her slaves well. She had only one daughter, Miss Betsey, for whom I was purchased, and who was about my own age. I was made quite a pet of by Miss Betsey, and loved her very much. She used to lead me about by the hand, and call me her little nigger. This was the happiest period of my life; for I was too young to understand rightly my condition as a slave, and too thoughtless and full of spirits to look forward to the days of toil and sorrow.

My mother was a household slave in the same family. I was under her own care, and my little brothers and sisters were my play-fellows and companions. My mother had

several fine children after she came to Mrs. Williams, –
three girls and two boys. The tasks given out to us
children were light, and we used to play together with
Miss Betsey, with as much freedom almost as if she had
been our sister.

My master, however, was a very harsh, selfish man;
and we always dreaded his return from sea. His wife was
herself much afraid of him; and, during his stay at home,
seldom dared to shew her usual kindness to the slaves. He
often left her, in the most distressed circumstances, to
reside in other female society, at some place in the West
Indies of which I have forgot the name. My poor mistress
bore his ill-treatment with great patience, and all her
slaves loved and pitied her. I was truly attached to her,
and, next to my own mother, loved her better than any
creature in the world. My obedience to her commands
was cheerfully given: it sprung solely from the affection I
felt for her, and not from fear of the power which the
white people's law had given her over me.

I had scarcely reached my twelfth year when my
mistress became too poor to keep so many of us at home;
and she hired me out to Mrs. Pruden, a lady who lived
about five miles off, in the adjoining parish, in a large
house near the sea. I cried bitterly at parting with my dear
mistress and Miss Betsey, and when I kissed my mother
and brothers and sisters, I thought my young heart would
break, it pained me so. But there was no help; I was
forced to go. Good Mrs. Williams comforted me by
saying that I should still be near the home I was about to
quit, and might come over and see her and my kindred
whenever I could obtain leave of absence from Mrs.
Pruden. A few hours after this I was taken to a strange
house, and found myself among strange people. This
separation seemed a sore trial to me then; but oh! 'twas
light, light to the trials I have since endured! – 'twas
nothing – nothing to be mentioned with them; but I was

a child then, and it was according to my strength.

I knew that Mrs. Williams could no longer maintain me; that she was fain to part with me for my food and clothing; and I tried to submit myself to the change. My new mistress was a passionate woman; but yet she did not treat me very unkindly. I do not remember her striking me but once, and that was for going to see Mrs. Williams when I heard she was sick, and staying longer than she had given me leave to do. All my employment at this time was nursing a sweet baby, little Master Daniel; and I grew so fond of my nursling that it was my greatest delight to walk out with him by the sea-shore, accompanied by his brother and sister, Miss Fanny and Master James. – Dear Miss Fanny! She was a sweet, kind young lady, and so fond of me that she wished me to learn all that she knew herself; and her method of teaching me was as follows: – Directly she had said her lessons to her grandmamma, she used to come running to me, and make me repeat them one by one after her; and in a few months I was able not only to say my letters but to spell many small words. But this happy state was not to last long. Those days were too pleasant to last. My heart always softens when I think of them.

At this time Mrs. Williams died. I was told suddenly of her death, and my grief was so great that, forgetting I had the baby in my arms, I ran away directly to my poor mistress's house; but reached it only in time to see the corpse carried out. Oh, that was a day of sorrow – a heavy day! All the slaves cried. My mother cried and lamented her sore; and I (foolish creature!) vainly entreated them to bring my dear mistress back to life. I knew nothing rightly about death then, and it seemed a hard thing to bear. When I thought about my mistress I felt as if the world was all gone wrong; and for many days and weeks I could think of nothing else. I returned to Mrs. Pruden's; but my sorrow was too great to be comforted, for my own dear mistress was always in my mind. Whether in the house or abroad, my thoughts were always talking to me about her.

I staid at Mrs. Pruden's about three months after this; I was then sent back to Mr. Williams to be sold. Oh, that was a sad sad time! I recollect the day well. Mrs. Pruden came to me and said, 'Mary, you will have to go home directly; your master is going to be married, and he means to sell you and two of your sisters to raise money for the wedding.' Hearing this I burst out a crying, – though I was then far from being sensible of the full weight of my misfortune, or of the misery that waited for me. Besides, I did not like to leave Mrs. Pruden, and the dear baby, who had grown very fond of me. For some time I could scarcely believe that Mrs. Pruden was in earnest, till I received orders for my immediate return. – Dear Miss Fanny! how she cried at parting with me, whilst I kissed and hugged the baby, thinking I should never see him again. I left Mrs. Pruden's, and walked home with a heart full of sorrow. The idea of being sold away from my mother and Miss Betsey was so frightful, that I dared not trust myself to think about it. We had been bought of Mrs. Myners, as I have mentioned, by Miss Betsey's grandfather, and given to her, so that we were by right *her* property, and I never thought we should be separated or sold away from her.

When I reached the house, I went in directly to Miss Betsey. I found her in great distress; and she cried out as soon as she saw me, 'Oh, Mary! my father is going to sell you all to raise money to marry that wicked woman. You are *my* slaves, and he has no right to sell you; but it is all to please her.' She then told me that my mother was living with her father's sister at a house close by, and I went there to see her. It was a sorrowful meeting; and we lamented with a great and sore crying our unfortunate situation. 'Here comes one of my poor piccaninnies!' she said, the moment I came in, 'one of the poor slave-brood who are to be sold to-morrow.'

Oh dear! I cannot bear to think of that day, – it is too much. – It recalls the great grief that filled my heart, and the woeful thoughts that passed to and fro through my mind, whilst listening to the pitiful words of my poor mother, weeping for the loss of her children. I wish I could find words to tell you all I then felt and suffered. The great God above alone knows the thoughts of the poor slave's heart, and the bitter pains which follow such separations as these. All that we love taken away from us – oh, it is sad, sad! and sore to be borne! – I got no sleep that night for thinking of the morrow; and dear Miss Betsey was scarcely less distressed. She could not bear to part with her old playmates and she cried sore and would not be pacified.

The black morning at length came; it came too soon for my poor mother and us. Whilst she was putting on us the new osnaburgs in which we were to be sold, she said, in a sorrowful voice, (I shall never forget it!) 'See, I am *shrouding* my poor children; what a task for a mother!' – She then called Miss Betsey to take leave of us. 'I am going to carry my little chickens to market,' (these were her very words) 'take your last look of them; may be you will see them no more.' 'Oh, my poor slaves! my own slaves!' said dear Miss Betsey, 'you belong to me; and it grieves my heart to part with you.' – Miss Betsey kissed us all, and, when she left us, my mother called the rest of the slaves to bid us good bye. One of them, a woman named Moll, came with her infant in her arms. 'Ay!' said my mother, seeing her turn away and look at her child with the tears in her eyes, 'your turn will come next.' The slaves could say nothing to comfort us; they could only weep and lament with us. When I left my dear little brothers and the house in which I had been brought up, I thought my heart would burst.

Our mother, weeping as she went, called me away with the children Hannah and Dinah, and we took the road that led to Hamble Town, which we reached about four o'clock in the afternoon. We followed my mother to the market-place, where she placed us in a row against a large house, with our backs to the wall and our arms folded across our breasts. I, as the eldest, stood first, Hannah next to me, then Dinah; and our mother stood beside, crying over us. My heart throbbed with grief and terror so violently, that I pressed my hands quite tightly across my breast, but I could not keep it still, and it continued to leap as though it would burst out of my body. But who cared for that? Did one of the many bystanders, who were looking at us so carelessly, think of the pain that wrung the hearts of the negro woman and her young ones? No, no! They were not all bad, I dare say, but slavery hardens white people's hearts towards the blacks; and many of them were not slow to make their remarks upon us aloud, without regard to our grief – though their light words fell like cayenne on the fresh wounds of our hearts. Oh those white people have small hearts who can only feel for themselves.

At length the vendue master, who was to offer us for sale like sheep or cattle, arrived, and asked my mother which was the eldest. She said nothing, but pointed to me. He took me by the hand, and led me out into the middle of the street, and, turning me slowly round, exposed me to the view of those who attended the vendue. I was soon surrounded by strange men, who examined and handled me in the same manner that a butcher would a calf or a lamb he was about to purchase, and who talked about my shape and size in like words – as if I could no more understand their meaning than the dumb beasts. I was then put up for sale. The bidding commenced at a few pounds, and gradually rose to fifty-seven,* when I was knocked down to the highest bidder; and the people who stood by said that I had fetched a great sum for so young a slave.

I then saw my sisters led forth, and sold to different owners; so that we had not the sad satisfaction of being partners in bondage. When the sale was over, my mother hugged and kissed us, and mourned over us, begging of us to keep up a good heart, and do our duty to our new masters. It was a sad parting; one went one way, one another, and our poor mammy went home with nothing.†

My new master was a Captain I—, who lived at Spanish Point. After parting with my mother and sisters, I followed him to his store, and he gave me into the charge of his son, a lad about my own age, Master Benjy, who

*Bermuda currency; about £38 sterling.

†Let the reader compare the above affecting account, taken down from the mouth of this negro woman, with the following description of a vendue of slaves at the Cape of Good Hope, published by me in 1826, from the letter of a friend, – and mark their similarity in several characteristic circumstances. The resemblance is easily accounted for: slavery wherever it prevails produces similar effects. – 'Having heard that there was to be a sale of cattle, farm stock, &c. by auction, at a Veld-Cornet's in the vicinity, we halted our waggon one day for the purpose of procuring a fresh spann of oxen. Among the stock of the farm sold, was a female slave and her three children. The two oldest children were girls, the one about thirteen years of age, and the other about eleven; the youngest was a boy. The whole family were exhibited together, but they were sold separately, and to different purchasers. The farmers examined them as if they had been so many head of cattle. While the sale was going on, the mother and her children were exhibited on a table, that they might be seen by the company, which was very large. There could not have been a finer subject for an able painter than this unhappy group. The tears, the anxiety, the anguish of the mother, while she met the gaze of the multitude, eyed the different countenances of the bidders, or cast a heart-rending look upon the children; and the simplicity and touching sorrow of the young ones, while they clung to their distracted parent, wiping their eyes, and half concealing their faces, – contrasted with the marked insensibility and jocular countenances of the spectators and purchasers, – furnished a striking commentary on the miseries of slavery, and its debasing effects upon the hearts of its abettors. While the woman was in this distressed situation she was asked, "Can you feed sheep?" Her reply was so indistinct that it escaped me; but it was probably in the negative, for her purchaser rejoined, in a loud and harsh voice, "Then I will teach you with the sjamboc," (a whip made of the rhinoceros' hide.) The mother and her three children were sold to three separate purchasers; and they were literally torn from each other.' – *Ed.*

took me to my new home. I did not know where I was going, or what my new master would do with me. My heart was quite broken with grief, and my thoughts went back continually to those from whom I had been so suddenly parted. 'Oh, my mother! my mother!' I kept saying to myself, 'Oh, my mammy and my sisters and my brothers, shall I never see you again!'

Oh, the trials! the trials! they make the salt water come into my eyes when I think of the days in which I was afflicted – the times that are gone; when I mourned and grieved with a young heart for those whom I loved.

It was night when I reached my new home. The house was large, and built at the bottom of a very high hill; but I could not see much of it that night. I saw too much of it afterwards. The stones and the timber were the best things in it; they were not so hard as the hearts of the owners.*

Before I entered the house, two slave women, hired from another owner, who were at work in the yard, spoke to me, and asked who I belonged to? I replied, 'I am come to live here.' 'Poor child, poor child!' they both said; 'you must keep a good heart, if you are to live here.' – When I went in, I stood up crying in a corner. Mrs. I— came and took off my hat, a little black silk hat Miss Pruden made for me, and said in a rough voice, 'You are not come here to stand up in corners and cry, you are come here to work.' She then put a child into my arms, and, tired as I was, I was forced instantly to take up my old occupation of a nurse. – I could not bear to look at my mistress, her countenance was so stern. She was a stout tall woman with a very dark complexion, and her brows were always drawn together into a frown. I thought of the words of the two slave women when I saw Mrs. I—, and heard the harsh sound of her voice.

*These strong expressions, and all of a similar character in this little narrative, are given verbatim as uttered by Mary Prince. – *Ed.*

The person I took the most notice of that night was a French Black called Hetty, whom my master took in privateering from another vessel, and made his slave. She was the most active woman I ever saw, and she was tasked to her utmost. A few minutes after my arrival she came in from milking the cows, and put the sweet-potatoes on for supper. She then fetched home the sheep, and penned them in the fold; drove home the cattle, and staked them about the pond side;* fed and rubbed down my master's horse, and gave the hog and the fed cow† their suppers; prepared the beds, and undressed the children, and laid them to sleep. I liked to look at her and watch all her doings, for her's was the only friendly face I had as yet seen, and I felt glad that she was there. She gave me my supper of potatoes and milk, and a blanket to sleep upon, which she spread for me in the passage before the door of Mrs. I—'s chamber.

I got a sad fright, that night. I was just going to sleep, when I heard a noise in my mistress's room; and she presently called out to inquire if some work was finished that she had ordered Hetty to do. 'No, Ma'am, not yet,' was Hetty's answer from below. On hearing this, my master started up from his bed, and just as he was, in his shirt, ran down stairs with a long cow-skin‡ in his hand. I heard immediately after, the cracking of the thong, and the house rang to the shrieks of poor Hetty, who kept crying out, 'Oh, Massa! Massa! me dead. Massa! have mercy upon me – don't kill me outright.' – This was a sad beginning for me. I sat up upon my blanket, trembling with terror, like a frightened hound, and thinking that my turn would come next. At length the house became still, and I forgot for a little while all my sorrows by falling fast asleep.

*The cattle on a small plantation in Bermuda are, it seems, often thus staked or tethered, both night and day, in situations where grass abounds.

†A cow fed for slaughter.

‡A thong of hard twisted hide, known by this name in the West Indies.

The next morning my mistress set about instructing me in my tasks. She taught me to do all sorts of household work; to wash and bake, pick cotton and wool, and wash floors, and cook. And she taught me (how can I ever forget it!) more things than these; she caused me to know the exact difference between the smart of the rope, the cart-whip, and the cow-skin, when applied to my naked body by her own cruel hand. And there was scarcely any punishment more dreadful than the blows I received on my face and head from her hard heavy fist. She was a fearful woman, and a savage mistress to her slaves.

There were two little slave boys in the house, on whom she vented her bad temper in a special manner. One of these children was a mulatto, called Cyrus, who had been bought while an infant in his mother's arms; the other, Jack, was an African from the coast of Guinea, whom a sailor had given or sold to my master. Seldom a day passed without these boys receiving the most severe treatment, and often for no fault at all. Both my master and mistress seemed to think that they had a right to ill-use them at their pleasure; and very often accompanied their commands with blows, whether the children were behaving well or ill. I have seen their flesh ragged and raw with licks. – Lick – lick – they were never secure one moment from a blow, and their lives were passed in continual fear. My mistress was not contented with using the whip, but often pinched their cheeks and arms in the most cruel manner. My pity for these poor boys was soon transferred to myself; for I was licked, and flogged, and pinched by her pitiless fingers in the neck and arms, exactly as they were. To strip me naked – to hang me up by the wrists and lay my flesh open with the cow-skin, was an ordinary punishment for even a slight offence. My mistress often robbed me too of the hours that belong to sleep. She used to sit up very late, frequently even until morning; and I had then to stand at a bench and wash during the greater part of the night, or pick wool and cotton and often I have dropped down overcome by sleep and fatigue, till roused from a state of stupor by the whip, and forced to start up to my tasks.

Poor Hetty, my fellow slave, was very kind to me, and I used to call her my Aunt; but she led a most miserable life, and her death was hastened (at least the slaves all believed and said so,) by the dreadful chastisement she received from my master during her pregnancy. It happened as follows. One of the cows had dragged the rope away from the stake to which Hetty had fastened it, and got loose. My master flew into a terrible passion, and ordered the poor creature to be stripped quite naked, notwithstanding her pregnancy, and to be tied up to a tree in the yard. He then flogged her as hard as he could lick, both with the whip and cow-skin, till she was all over streaming with blood. He rested, and then beat her again and again. Her shrieks were terrible. The consequence was that poor Hetty was brought to bed before her time, and was delivered after severe labour of a dead child. She appeared to recover after her confinement, so far that she was repeatedly flogged by both master and mistress afterwards; but her former strength never returned to her. Ere long her body and limbs swelled to a great size; and she lay on a mat in the kitchen, till the water burst out of her body and she died. All the slaves said that death was a good thing for poor Hetty; but I cried very much for her death. The manner of it filled me with horror. I could not bear to think about it; yet it was always present to my mind for many a day.

After Hetty died all her labours fell upon me, in addition to my own. I had now to milk eleven cows every morning before sunrise, sitting among the damp weeds; to take care of the cattle as well as the children; and to do the work of the house. There was no end to my toils – no end to my blows. I lay down at night and rose up in the morning in fear and sorrow; and often wished that like poor Hetty I could escape from this cruel bondage and be at rest in the grave. But the hand of that God whom then I knew not, was stretched over me; and I was mercifully preserved for better things. It was then, however, my heavy lot to weep, weep, weep, and that for years; to pass from one misery to another, and from one cruel master to a worse. But I must go on with the thread of my story.

One day a heavy squall of wind and rain came on suddenly, and my mistress sent me round the corner of the house to empty a large earthen jar. The jar was already cracked with an old deep crack that divided it in the middle, and in turning it upside down to empty it, it parted in my hand. I could not help the accident, but I was dreadfully frightened, looking forward to a severe punishment. I ran crying to my mistress, 'O mistress, the jar has come in two.' 'You have broken it, have you?' she replied; 'come directly here to me.' I came trembling: she stripped and flogged me long and severely with the cow-skin; as long as she had strength to use the lash, for she did not give over till she was quite tired. – When my master came home at night, she told him of my fault; and oh, frightful! how he fell a swearing. After abusing me with every ill name he could think of, (too, too bad to speak in England,) and giving me several heavy blows with his hand, he said, 'I shall come home to-morrow morning at twelve, on purpose to give you a round hundred.' He kept his word – Oh sad for me! I cannot easily forget it. He tied me up upon a ladder, and gave me a hundred lashes with his own hand, and master Benjy stood by to count them for him. When he had licked me for some time he sat down to take breath; then after resting, he beat me again and again, until he was quite wearied, and so hot (for the weather was very sultry), that he sank back in his chair, almost like to faint. While my mistress went to bring him drink, there was a dreadful earthquake. Part of the roof fell down, and every thing in the house went – clatter, clatter, clatter. Oh I thought the end of all things near at hand; and I was so sore with the flogging, that I scarcely cared whether I lived or died. The earth was groaning and shaking; every thing tumbling about; and my mistress and the slaves were shrieking and crying out, 'The earthquake! the earthquake!' It was an awful day for us all.

During the confusion I crawled away on my hands and knees, and laid myself down under the steps of the piazza, in front of the house. I was in a dreadful state – my body all blood and bruises, and I could not help moaning piteously. The other slaves, when they saw me, shook their heads and said, 'Poor child! poor child' – I lay there till the morning, careless of what might happen, for life was very weak in me, and I wished more than ever to die. But when we are very young, death always seems a great way off, and it would not come that night to me. The next morning I was forced by my master to rise and go about my usual work, though my body and limbs were so stiff and sore, that I could not move without the greatest pain. – Nevertheless, even after all this severe punishment, I never heard the last of that jar; my mistress was always throwing it in my face.

Some little time after this, one of the cows got loose from the stake, and eat one of the sweet-potatoe slips. I was milking when my master found it out. He came to me, and without any more ado, stooped down, and taking off his heavy boot, he struck me such a severe blow in the small of my back, that I shrieked with agony, and thought I was killed; and I feel a weakness in that part to this day. The cow was frightened by his violence, and kicked down the pail and spilt the milk all about. My master knew that this accident was his own fault, but he was so enraged that he seemed glad of an excuse to go on with his ill usage. I cannot remember how many licks he gave me then, but he beat me till I was unable to stand, and till he himself was weary.

After this I ran away and went to my mother, who was living with Mr. Richard Darrel. My poor mother was both grieved and glad to see me; grieved because I had been so ill used, and glad because she had not seen me for a long, long while. She dared not receive me into the house, but she hid me up in a hole in the rocks near, and brought me food at night, after every body was asleep. My father, who lived at Crow-Lane, over the salt-water channel, at last heard of my being hid up in the cavern, and he came and took me back to my master. Oh I was loth, loth to go back; but as there was no remedy, I was obliged to submit.

When we got home, my poor father said to Capt. I—, 'Sir, I am sorry that my child should be forced to run away from her owner; but the treatment she has received is enough to break her heart. The sight of her wounds has nearly broke mine. – I entreat you, for the love of God, to forgive her for running away, and that you will be a kind master to her in future.' Capt. I— said I was used as well as I deserved, and that I ought to be punished for running away. I then took courage and said that I could stand the floggings no longer; that I was weary of my life, and therefore I had run away to my mother; but mothers could only weep and mourn over their children, they could not save them from cruel masters – from the whip, the rope, and the cow-skin. He told me to hold my tongue and go about my work, or he would find a way to settle me. He did not, however, flog me that day.

For five years after this I remained in his house, and almost daily received the same harsh treatment. At length he put me on board a sloop, and to my great joy sent me away to Turk's Island. I was not permitted to see my mother or father, or poor sisters and brothers, to say good bye, though going away to a strange land, and might never see them again. Oh the Buckra people who keep slaves think that black people are like cattle, without natural affection. But my heart tells me it is far otherwise.

We were nearly four weeks on the voyage, which was unusually long. Sometimes we had a light breeze, sometimes a great calm, and the ship made no way; so that our provisions and water ran very low, and we were put upon short allowance. I should almost have been starved had it not been for the kindness of a black man called Anthony, and his wife, who had brought their own victuals, and shared them with me.

When we went ashore at the Grand Quay, the captain sent me to the house of my new master, Mr. D—, to whom Captain I— had sold me. Grand Quay is a small town upon a sandbank; the houses low and built of wood. Such was my new master's. The first person I saw, on my arrival, was Mr. D—, a stout sulky looking man, who carried me through the hall to show me to his wife and children. Next day I was put up by the vendue master to know how much I was worth, and I was valued at one hundred pounds currency.

My new master was one of the owners or holders of the salt ponds, and he received a certain sum for every slave that worked upon his premises, whether they were young or old. This sum was allowed him out of the profits arising from the salt works. I was immediately sent to work in the salt water with the rest of the slaves. This work was perfectly new to me. I was given a half barrel and a shovel, and had to stand up to my knees in the water, from four o'clock in the morning till nine, when we were given some Indian corn boiled in water, which we were obliged to swallow as fast as we could for fear the rain should come on and melt the salt. We were then called again to our tasks, and worked through the heat of the day; the sun flaming upon our heads like fire, and raising salt blisters in those parts which were not completely covered. Our feet and legs, from standing in the salt water for so many hours, soon became full of dreadful boils, which eat down in some cases to the very bone, afflicting the sufferers with great torment. We came home at twelve; ate our corn soup, called *blawly*, as fast as we could, and went back to our employment till dark at night. We then shovelled up the salt in large heaps, and went down to the sea, where we washed the pickle from our limbs, and cleaned the barrows and shovels from the salt. When we returned to the house, our master gave us each our allowance of raw Indian corn, which we pounded in a mortar and boiled in water for our suppers.

We slept in a long shed, divided into narrow slips, like the stalls used for cattle. Boards fixed upon stakes driven into the ground, without mat or covering, were our only beds. On Sundays, after we had washed the salt bags, and done other work required of us, we went into the bush and cut the long soft grass, of which we made trusses for our legs and feet to rest upon, for they were so full of the salt boils that we could get no rest lying upon the bare boards.

Though we worked from morning till night, there was no satisfying Mr. D—. I hoped, when I left Capt. I—, that I should have been better off, but I found it was but going from one butcher to another. There was this difference between them: my former master used to beat me while raging and foaming with passion; Mr. D— was usually quite calm. He would stand by and give orders for a slave to be cruelly whipped, and assist in the punishment, without moving a muscle of his face; walking about and taking snuff with the greatest composure. Nothing could touch his hard heart – neither sighs, nor tears, nor prayers, nor streaming blood; he was deaf to our cries, and careless of our sufferings. – Mr. D— has often stripped me naked, hung me up by the wrists, and beat me with the cow-skin, with his own hand, till my body was raw with gashes. Yet there was nothing very remarkable in this; for it might serve as a sample of the common usage of the slaves on that horrible island.

Owing to the boils in my feet, I was unable to wheel the barrow fast through the sand, which got into the sores, and made me stumble at every step; and my master, having no pity for my sufferings from this cause, rendered them far more intolerable, by chastising me for not being able to move so fast as he wished me. Another of our employments was to row a little way off from the shore in a boat, and dive for large stones to build a wall round our master's house. This was very hard work; and the great waves breaking over us continually, made us often so giddy that we lost our footing, and were in danger of being drowned.

Ah, poor me! – my tasks were never ended. Sick or well, it was work – work –work! – After the diving season was over, we were sent to the South Creek, with large bills, to cut up mangoes to burn lime with. Whilst one party of slaves were thus employed, another were sent to the other side of the island to break up coral out of the sea.

When we were ill, let our complaint be what it might, the only medicine given to us was a great bowl of hot salt water, with salt mixed with it, which made us very sick. If we could not keep up with the rest of the gang of slaves, we were put in the stocks, and severely flogged the next morning. Yet, not the less, our master expected, after we had thus been kept from our rest, and our limbs rendered stiff and sore with ill usage, that we should still go through the ordinary tasks of the day all the same. – Sometimes we had to work all night, measuring salt to load a vessel; or turning a machine to draw water out of the sea for the salt-making. Then we had no sleep – no rest – but were forced to work as fast as we could, and go on again all next day the same as usual. Work – work –

work – Oh that Turk's Island was a horrible place! The people in England, I am sure, have never found out what is carried on there. Cruel, horrible place!

Mr. D— had a slave called old Daniel, whom he used to treat in the most cruel manner. Poor Daniel was lame in the hip, and could not keep up with the rest of the slaves; and our master would order him to be stripped and laid down on the ground, and have him beaten with a rod of rough briar till his skin was quite red and raw. He would then call for a bucket of salt, and fling upon the raw flesh till the man writhed on the ground like a worm, and screamed aloud with agony. This poor man's wounds were never healed, and I have often seen them full of maggots, which increased his torments to an intolerable degree. He was an object of pity and terror to the whole gang of slaves, and in his wretched case we saw, each of us, our own lot, if we should live to be as old.

Oh the horrors of slavery! – How the thought of it pains my heart! But the truth ought to be told of it; and what my eyes have seen I think it is my duty to relate; for few people in England know what slavery is. I have been a slave – I have felt what a slave feels, and I know what a slave knows; and I would have all the good people in England to know it too, that they may break our chains, and set us free.

Mr. D— had another slave called Ben. He being very hungry, stole a little rice one night after he came in from work, and cooked it for his supper. But his master soon discovered the theft; locked him up all night; and kept him without food till one o'clock the next day. He then hung Ben up by his hands, and beat him from time to time till the slaves came in at night. We found the poor creature hung up when we came home; with a pool of blood beneath him, and our master still licking him. but this was not the worst. My master's son was in the habit of stealing the rice and rum. Ben had seen him do this, and thought he might do the same, and when master found out that Ben had stolen the rice and swore to punish him, he tried to excuse himself by saying that Master Dickey did the same thing every night. The lad denied it to his father, and was so angry with Ben for informing against him, that out of revenge he ran and got a bayonet, and whilst the poor wretch was suspended by his hands and writhing under his wounds, he run it quite through his foot. I was not by when he did it, but I saw the wound when I came home, and heard Ben tell the manner in which it was done.

I must say something more about this cruel son of a cruel father. – He had no heart – no fear of God; he had been brought up by a bad father in a bad path, and he delighted to follow in the same steps. There was a little old woman among the slaves called Sarah, who was nearly past work; and, Master Dickey being the overseer of the slaves just then, this poor creature, who was subject to several bodily infirmities, and was not quite right in her head, did not wheel the barrow fast enough to please him. He threw her down on the ground, and after beating her severely, he took her up in his arms and flung her among the prickly-pear bushes, which are all covered over with sharp venomous prickles. By this her naked flesh was so grievously wounded, that her body swelled and festered all over, and she died in a few days after. In telling my own sorrows, I cannot pass by those of my fellow-slaves – for when I think of my own griefs, I remember theirs.

I think it was about ten years I had worked in the salt ponds at Turk's Island, when my master left off business, and retired to a house he had in Bermuda, leaving his son to succeed him in the island. He took me with him to wait upon his daughters; and I was joyful, for I was sick, sick of Turk's Island, and my heart yearned to see my native place again, my mother, and my kindred.

I had seen my poor mother during the time I was a slave in Turk's Island. One Sunday morning I was on the beach with some of the slaves, and we saw a sloop come in loaded with slaves to work in the salt water. We got a boat and went aboard. When I came upon the deck I asked the black people, 'Is there any one here for me?' 'Yes,' they said, 'your mother.' I thought they said this in jest – I could scarcely believe them for joy; but when I saw my poor mammy my joy was turned to sorrow, for she had gone from her senses. 'Mammy,' I said, 'is this you!' She did not know me. 'Mammy,' I said, 'what's the matter?' She began to talk foolishly and said that she had been under the vessel's bottom. They had been overtaken by a violent storm at sea. My poor mother had never been on the sea before, and she was so ill, that she lost her senses, and it was long before she came quite to herself again. She had a sweet child with her – a little sister I had never seen, about four years of age, called Rebecca. I took her on shore with me, for I felt I should love her directly; and I kept her with me a week. Poor little thing! her's has been a sad life, and continues so to this day. My mother worked for some years on the island, but was taken back to Bermuda some time before my master carried me again thither.*

After I left Turk's Island, I was told by some negroes that came over from it, that the poor slaves had built up a place with boughs and leaves, where they might meet for prayers, but the white people pulled it down twice, and

*Of the subsequent lot of her relatives she can tell but little. She says, her father died while she and her mother were at Turk's Island; and that he had been long dead and buried before any of his children in Bermuda knew of it, they being slaves on other estates. Her mother died after Mary went to Antigua. Of the fate of the rest of her kindred, seven brothers and three sisters, she knows nothing further than this – that the eldest sister, who had several children to her master, was taken by him to Trinidad; and that the youngest, Rebecca, is still alive, and in slavery in Bermuda. Mary herself is now about forty-three years of age. – *Ed.*

would not allow them even a shed for prayers. A flood came down soon after and washed away many houses, filled the place with sand, and overflowed the ponds: and I do think that this was for their wickedness; for the Buckra men* there were very wicked. I saw and heard much that was very very bad at that place.

I was several years the slave of Mr. D— after I returned to my native place. Here I worked in the grounds. My work was planting and hoeing sweet-potatoes, Indian corn, plaintains, bananas, cabbages, pumpkins, onions, &c. I did all the household work, and attended upon a horse and cow besides, – going also upon all errands. I had to curry the horse – to clean and feed him – and sometimes to ride him a little. I had more than enough to do – but still it was not so very bad as Turk's Island.

My old master often got drunk, and then he would get in a fury with his daughter, and beat her till she was not fit to be seen. I remember on one occasion, I had gone to fetch water, and when I was coming up the hill I heard a great screaming; I ran as fast as I could to the house, put down the water, and went into the chamber, where I found my master beating Miss D— dreadfully. I strove with all my strength to get her away from him; for she was all black and blue with bruises. He had beat her with his fist, and almost killed her. The people gave me credit for getting her away. He turned round and began to lick me. Then I said, 'Sir, this is not Turk's Island.' I can't repeat his answer, the words were too wicked – too bad to say. He wanted to treat me the same in Bermuda as he had done in Turk's Island.

He had an ugly fashion of stripping himself quite naked and ordering me then to wash him in a tub of water. This was worse to me than all the licks. Sometimes when he called me to wash him I would not come, my eyes were so

---

*Negro term for white people.

full of shame. He would then come to beat me. One time I had plates and knives in my hand, and I dropped both plates and knives, and some of the plates were broken. He struck me so severely for this, that at last I defended myself, for I thought it was high time to do so. I then told him I would not live longer with him, for he was a very indecent man – very spiteful, and too indecent; with no shame for his servants, no shame for his own flesh. So I went away to a neighbouring house and sat down and cried till the next morning, when I went home again, not knowing what else to do.

After that I was hired to work at Cedar Hills, and every Saturday night I paid the money to my master. I had plenty of work to do there – plenty of washing; but yet I made myself pretty comfortable. I earned two dollars and a quarter a week, which is twenty pence a day.

During the time I worked there, I heard that Mr. John Wood was going to Antigua. I felt a great wish to go there, and I went to Mr. D—, and asked him to let me go in Mr. Wood's service. Mr. Wood did not then want to purchase me; it was my own fault that I came under him, I was so anxious to go. It was ordained to be, I suppose; God led me there. The truth is, I did not wish to be any longer the slave of my indecent master.

Mr. Wood took me with him to Antigua, to the town of St. John's, where he lived. This was about fifteen years ago. He did not then know whether I was to be sold; but Mrs. Wood found that I could work, and she wanted to buy me. Her husband then wrote to my master to inquire whether I was to be sold? Mr. D— wrote in reply, 'that I should not be sold to any one that would treat me ill.' It was strange he should say this, when he had treated me so ill himself. So I was purchased by Mr. Wood for 300 dollars (or £100 Bermuda currency.)*

---

*About £67.10s. sterling.

My work there was to attend the chambers and nurse the child, and to go down to the pond and wash clothes. But I soon fell ill of the rheumatism, and grew so very lame that I was forced to walk with a stick. I got the Saint Anthony's fire, also, in my left leg, and became quite a cripple. No one cared much to come near me, and I was ill a long long time; for several months I could not lift the limb. I had to lie in a little old out-house, that was swarming with bugs and other vermin, which tormented me greatly; but I had no other place to lie in. I got the rheumatism by catching cold at the pond side, from washing in the fresh water; in the salt water I never got cold. The person who lived in next yard, (a Mrs. Greene,) could not bear to hear my cries and groans. She was kind, and used to send an old slave woman to help me, who sometimes brought me a little soup. When the doctor found I was so ill, he said I must be put into a bath of hot water. The old slave got the bark of some bush that was good for pains, which she boiled in the hot water, and every night she came and put me into the bath, and did what she could for me; I don't know what I should have done, or what would have become of me, had it not been for her. – My mistress, it is true, did send me a little food; but no one from our family came near me but the cook, who used to shove my food in at the door, and say, 'Molly, Molly, there's your dinner.' My mistress did not care to take any trouble about me; and if the Lord had not put it into the hearts of the neighbours to be kind to me, I must, I really think, have lain and died.

It was a long time before I got well enough to work in the house. Mrs. Wood, in the meanwhile, hired a mulatto woman to nurse the child; but she was such a fine lady she wanted to be mistress over me. I thought it very hard for a coloured woman to have rule over me because I was a slave and she was free. Her name was Martha Wilcox; she was a saucy woman, very saucy; and she went and complained of me, without cause, to my mistress, and made her angry with me. Mrs. Wood told me that if I did not mind what I was about, she would get my master to strip me and give me fifty lashes: 'You have been used to the whip,' she said, 'and you shall have it here.' This was the first time she threatened to have me flogged; and she gave me the threatening so strong of what she would have done to me, that I thought I should have fallen down at her feet, I was so vexed and hurt by her words. The mulatto woman was rejoiced to have power to keep me down. She was constantly making mischief; there was no living for the slaves – no peace after she came.

I was also sent by Mrs. Wood to be put in the Cage one night, and was next morning flogged, by the magistrate's order, at her desire; and this all for a quarrel I had about a pig with another slave woman. I was flogged on my naked back on this occasion; although I was in no fault after all; for old Justice Dyett, when we came before him, said that I was in the right, and ordered the pig to be given to me. This was about two or three years after I came to Antigua.

When we moved from the middle of the town to the Point, I used to be in the house and do all the work and mind the children, though still very ill with the rheumatism. Every week I had to wash two large bundles of clothes, as much as a boy could help me to lift; but I could give no satisfaction. My mistress was always abusing and fretting after me. It is not possible to tell all her ill language. – One day she followed me foot after foot scolding and rating me. I bore in silence a great deal of ill words: at last my heart was quite full, and I told her that she ought not to use me so; – that when I was ill I might have lain and died for what she cared; and no one would then come near me to nurse me, because they were afraid of my mistress. This was a great affront. She called her husband and told him what I had said. He flew into a passion: but did not beat me then; he only abused and swore at me; and then gave me a note and bade me go and look for an owner. Not that he meant to sell me; but he did this to please his wife and to frighten me. I went to Adam White, a cooper, a free black who had money, and asked him to buy me. He went directly to Mr. Wood, but was informed that I was not to be sold. The next day my master whipped me.

Another time (about five years ago) my mistress got vexed with me because I fell sick and I could not keep on with my work. She complained to her husband, and he sent me off again to look for an owner. I went to a Mr. Burchell, showed him the note, and asked him to buy me for my own benefit; for I had saved about 100 dollars, and hoped with a little help, to purchase my freedom. He accordingly went to my master: – 'Mr. Wood,' he said, 'Molly has brought me a note that she wants an owner. If you intend to sell her, I may as well buy her as another.' My master put him off and said that he did not mean to sell me. I was very sorry at this, for I had no comfort with Mrs. Wood, and I wished greatly to get my freedom.

The way in which I made my money was this. – When my master and mistress went from home, as they sometimes did, and left me to take care of the house and premises, I had a good deal of time to myself and made the most of it. I took in washing, and sold coffee and yams and other provisions to the captains of ships. I did not sit still idling during the absence of my owners; for I wanted, by all honest means, to earn money to buy my freedom. Sometimes I bought a hog cheap on board ship, and sold it for double the money on shore; and I also earned a good deal by selling coffee. By this means I by degrees acquired a little cash. A gentleman also lent me some to help to buy my freedom – but when I could not get free he got it back again. His name was Captain Abbot.

My master and mistress went on one occasion into the country, to Date Hill, for a change of air, and carried me with them to take charge of the children, and to do the work of the house. While I was in the country, I saw how the field negroes are worked in Antigua. They are worked very hard and fed but scantily. They are called out to work before daybreak, and come home after dark; and then each has to heave his bundle of grass for the cattle in the pen. Then, on Sunday morning, each slave has to go out and gather a large bundle of grass; and, when they bring it home, they have all to sit at the manager's door and wait till he comes out: often have they to wait there till past eleven o'clock without any breakfast. After that, those that have yams or potatoes, or fire-wood to sell, hasten to market to buy a dog's worth* of salt fish, or pork, which is a great treat for them. Some of them buy a little pickle out of the shad barrels, which they call sauce, to season their yams and Indian corn. It is very wrong, I know, to work on Sunday or go to market; but will not God call the Buckra men to answer for this on the great day of judgment – since they will give the slaves no other day?

While we were at Date Hill Christmas came; and the slave woman who had the care of the place (which then belonged to Mr. Roberts the marshal), asked me to go with her to her husband's house, to a Methodist meeting for prayer, at a plantation called Winthorps. I went; and they were the first prayers I ever understood. One woman prayed; and then they all sung a hymn; then there was another prayer and another hymn; and then they all spoke by turns of their own griefs as sinners. The husband of the woman I went with was a black driver. His name was Henry. He confessed that he had treated the slaves very cruelly; but said that he was compelled to

*A dog is the 72nd part of a dollar.

obey the orders of his master. He prayed them all to forgive him, and he prayed that God would forgive him. He said it was a horrid thing for a ranger† to have sometimes to beat his own wife or sister; but he must do so if ordered by his master.

I felt sorry for my sins also. I cried the whole night, but I was too much ashamed to speak. I prayed God to forgive me. This meeting had a great impression on my mind, and led my spirit to the Moravian church; so that when I got back to town, I went and prayed to have my name put down in the Missionaries' book; and I followed the church earnestly every opportunity. I did not then tell my mistress about it; for I knew that she would not give me leave to go. But I felt I *must* go. Whenever I carried the children their lunch at school, I ran round and went to hear the teachers.

The Moravian ladies (Mrs. Richter, Mrs. Olufsen, and Mrs. Sauter) taught me to read in the class; and I got on very fast. In this class there were all sorts of people, old and young, grey headed folks and children; but most of them were free people. After we had done spelling, we tried to read in the Bible. After the reading was over, the missionary gave out a hymn for us to sing. I dearly loved to go to the church, it was so solemn. I never knew rightly that I had much sin till I went there. When I found out that I was a great sinner, I was very sorely grieved, and very much frightened. I used to pray God to pardon my sins for Christ's sake, and forgive me for every thing I had done amiss; and when I went home to my work, I always thought about what I had heard from the missionaries, and wished to be good that I might go to heaven. After a while I was admitted a candidate for the holy Communion. – I had been baptized long before this, in August 1817, by the Rev. Mr. Curtin, of the English

†The head negro of an estate – a person who has the chief superintendence under the manager.

Church, after I had been taught to repeat the Creed and the Lord's Prayer. I wished at that time to attend a Sunday School taught by Mr. Curtin, but he would not receive me without a written note from my master, granting his permission. I did not ask my owner's permission, from the belief that it would be refused; so that I got no farther instruction at that time from the English Church.*

Some time after I began to attend the Moravian Church, I met with Daniel James, afterwards my dear husband. He was a carpenter and cooper to his trade; an honest, hard-working, decent black man, and a widower. He had purchased his freedom of his mistress, old Mrs. Baker, with money he had earned whilst a slave. When he asked me to marry him, I took time to consider the matter over with myself, and would not say yes till he went to church with me and joined the Moravians. He was very industrious after he bought his freedom; and he had hired a comfortable house, and had convenient things about him. We were joined in marriage, about Christmas 1826, in the Moravian Chapel at Spring Gardens, by the Rev. Mr. Olufsen. We could not be married in the English Church. English marriage is not allowed to slaves; and no free man can marry a slave woman.

When Mr. Wood heard of my marriage, he flew into a great rage, and sent for Daniel, who was helping to build a house for his old mistress. Mr. Wood asked him who gave him a right to marry a slave of his? My husband said, 'Sir, I am a free man, and thought I had a right to

*She possesses a copy of Mrs. Trimmer's 'Charity School Spelling Book,' presented to her by the Rev. Mr. Curtin, and dated August 30, 1817. In this book her name is written 'Mary, Princess of Wales' – an appellation which, she says, was given her by her owners. It is a common practice for the colonists to give ridiculous names of this description to their slaves; being, in fact, one of the numberless modes of expressing the habitual contempt with which they regard the negro race. – In printing this narrative we have retained Mary's paternal name of Prince. – *Ed.*

choose a wife; but if I had known Molly was not allowed to have a husband, I should not have asked her to marry me.' Mrs. Wood was more vexed about my marriage than her husband. She could not forgive me for getting married, but stirred up Mr. Wood to flog me dreadfully with his horsewhip. I thought it very hard to be whipped at my time of life for getting a husband – I told her so. She said that she would not have nigger men about the yards and premises, or allow a nigger man's clothes to be washed in the same tub where hers were washed. She was fearful, I think, that I should lose her time, in order to wash and do things for my husband: but I had then no time to wash for myself; I was obliged to put out my own clothes, though I was always at the wash-tub.

I had not much happiness in my marriage, owing to my being a slave. It made my husband sad to see me so ill-treated. Mrs. Wood was always abusing me about him. She did not lick me herself, but she got her husband to do it for her, whilst she fretted the flesh off my bones. Yet for all this she would not sell me. She sold five slaves whilst I was with her; but though she was always finding fault with me, she would not part with me. However, Mr. Wood afterwards allowed Daniel to have a place to live in our yard, which we were very thankful for.

After this, I fell ill again with the rheumatism, and was sick a long time; but whether sick or well, I had my work to do. About this time I asked my master and mistress to let me buy my own freedom. With the help of Mr. Burchell, I could have found the means to pay Mr. Wood; for it was agreed that I should afterwards serve Mr. Burchell a while, for the cash he was to advance for me. I was earnest in the request to my owners; but their hearts were hard – too hard to consent. Mrs. Wood was very angry – she grew quite outrageous – she called me a black devil, and asked me who had put freedom into my head. 'To be free is very sweet,' I said: but she took good care to keep me a slave. I saw her change colour, and I left the room.

About this time my master and mistress were going to England to put their son in school, and bring their daughters home; and they took me with them to take care of the child. I was willing to come to England: I thought that by going there I should probably get cured of my rheumatism, and should return with my master and mistress, quite well, to my husband. My husband was willing for me to come away, for he had heard that my master would free me, – and I also hoped this might prove true; but it was all a false report.

The steward of the ship was very kind to me. He and my husband were in the same class in the Moravian Church. I was thankful that he was so friendly, for my mistress was not kind to me on the passage; and she told me, when she was angry, that she did not intend to treat me any better in England than in the West Indies – that I need not expect it. And she was as good as her word.

When we drew near to England, the rheumatism seized all my limbs worse than ever, and my body was dreadfully swelled. When we landed at the Tower, I shewed my flesh to my mistress, but she took no great notice of it. We were obliged to stop at the tavern till my master got a house; and a day or two after, my mistress sent me down into the wash-house to learn to wash in the English way. In the West Indies we wash with cold water – in England with hot. I told my mistress I was afraid that putting my hands first into the hot water and then into the cold, would increase the pain in my limbs. The doctor had told my mistress long before I came from the West Indies, that I was a sickly body and the washing did not agree with me. But Mrs. Wood would not release me from the tub, so I was forced to do as I could. I grew worse, and could not stand to wash. I was then forced to sit down with the tub before me, and often through pain and weakness was reduced to kneel or to sit down on the floor, to finish my task. When I complained to my mistress of this, she only got into a passion as usual, and said washing in hot water could not hurt any one; – that I was lazy and insolent, and wanted to be free of my work; but that she would make me do it. I thought her very hard on me, and my heart rose up within me. However I kept still at that time, and went down again to wash the child's things; but the English washerwomen who were at work there, when they saw that I was so ill, had pity upon me and washed them for me.

After that, when we came up to live in Leigh Street, Mrs. Wood sorted out five bags of clothes which we had used at sea, and also such as had been worn since we came on shore, for me and the cook to wash. Elizabeth the cook told her, that she did not think that I was able to stand to the tub, and that she had better hire a woman. I also said myself, that I had come over to nurse the child, and that I was sorry I had come from Antigua, since mistress would work me so hard, without compassion for my rheumatism. Mr. and Mrs. Wood, when they heard this, rose up in a passion against me. They opened the door and bade me get out. But I was a stranger, and did not know one door in the street from another, and was unwilling to go away. They made a dreadful uproar, and from that day they constantly kept cursing and abusing me. I was obliged to wash, though I was very ill. Mrs. Wood, indeed once hired a washerwoman, but she was not well treated, and would come no more.

My master quarrelled with me another time, about one of our great washings, his wife having stirred him up to do so. He said he would compel me to do the whole of the washing given out to me, or if I again refused, he would take a short course with me: he would either send me down to the brig in the river, to carry me back to Antigua, or he would turn me at once out of doors, and let me provide for myself. I said I would willingly go back, if he would let me purchase my own freedom. But this enraged him more than all the rest: he cursed and swore at me dreadfully, and said he would never sell my freedom – if I wished to be free, I was free in England, and I might go and try what freedom would do for me, and be d—d. My heart was very sore with this treatment, but I had to go on. I continued to do my work, and did all I could to give satisfaction, but all would not do.

Shortly after, the cook left them, and then matters went on ten times worse. I always washed the child's clothes without being commanded to do it, and any thing else that was wanted in the family; though still I was very sick – very sick indeed. When the great washing came round, which was every two months, my mistress got together again a great many heavy things, such as bed-ticks, bed-coverlets, &c. for me to wash. I told her I was too ill to wash such heavy things that day. She said, she supposed I thought myself a free woman, but I was not; and if I did not do it directly I should be instantly turned out of doors. I stood a long time before I could answer, for I did not know well what to do. I knew that I was free in England, but I did not know where to go, or how to get my living; and therefore, I did not like to leave the house. But Mr. Wood said he would send for a constable to thrust me out; and at last I took courage and resolved that I would not be longer thus treated, but would go and trust to Providence. This was the fourth time they had threatened to turn me out, and, go where I might, I was determined now to take them at their word; though I thought it very hard, after I had lived with them for thirteen years, and worked for them like a horse, to be driven out in this way, like a beggar. My only fault was being sick, and therefore unable to please my mistress, who thought she never could get work enough out of her slaves; and I told them so: but they only abused me and drove me out. This took place from two to three months, I think, after we came to England.

When I came away, I went to the man (one Mash) who used to black the shoes of the family, and asked his wife to get somebody to go with me to Hatton Garden to the Moravian Missionaries: these were the only persons I knew in England. The woman sent a young girl with me to the mission house, and I saw there a gentleman called Mr. Moore. I told him my whole story, and how my owners had treated me, and asked him to take in my truck with what few clothes I had. The missionaries were very kind to me – they were sorry for my destitute situation, and gave me leave to bring my things to be placed under their care. They were very good people, and they told me to come to the church.

When I went back to Mr. Wood's to get my trunk, I saw a lady, Mrs. Pell, who was on a visit to my mistress. When Mr. and Mrs. Wood heard me come in, they set this lady to stop me, finding that they had gone too far with me. Mrs. Pell came out to me, and said, 'Are you really going to leave, Molly? Don't leave, but come into the country with me.' I believe she said this because she thought Mrs. Wood would easily get me back again. I replied to her, 'Ma'am, this is the fourth time my master and mistress have driven me out, or threatened to drive me – and I will give them no more occasion to bid me go. I was not willing to leave them, for I am a stranger in this country, but now I must go – I can stay no longer to be used.' Mrs. Pell then went up stairs to my mistress, and told that I would go, and that she could not stop me. Mrs. Wood was very much hurt and frightened when she found I was determined to go out that day. She said, 'If she goes the people will rob her, and then turn her adrift.' She did not say this to me, but she spoke it loud enough for me to hear; that it might induce me not to go, I suppose. Mr. Wood also asked me where I was going to. I told him where I had been, and that I should never have gone away had I not been driven out by my owners. He had given me a written paper some time before, which said that I had come with them to England by my own desire; and that was true. It said also that I left them of my own free will, because I was a free woman in England; and that I was idle and would not do my work – which was not true. I gave this paper afterwards to a gentleman who inquired into my case.*

I went into the kitchen and got my clothes out. The nurse and the servant girl were there, and I said to the man who was going to take out my trunk, 'Stop, before you take up this trunk, and hear what I have to say before these people. I am going out of this house, as I was ordered; but I have done no wrong at all to my owners, neither here nor in the West Indies. I always worked very hard to please them, both by night and day; but there was no giving satisfaction, for my mistress could never be satisfied with reasonable service. I told my mistress I was sick, and yet she has ordered me out of doors. This is the fourth time; and now I am going out.'

And so I came out, and went and carried my trunk to the Moravians. I then returned back to Mash the shoe-black's house, and begged his wife to take me in. I had a little West Indian money in my trunk; and they got it changed for me. This helped to support me for a little while. The man's wife was very kind to me. I was very sick, and she boiled nourishing things up for me. She also sent for a doctor to see me, and sent me medicine, which did me good, though I was ill for a long time with the rheumatic pains. I lived a good many months with these poor people, and they nursed me, and did all that lay in their power to serve me. The man was well acquainted with my situation, as he used to go to and fro to Mr.

---

*See page 85.

Wood's house to clean shoes and knives; and he and his wife were sorry for me.

About this time, a woman of the name of Hill told me of the Anti-Slavery Society, and went with me to their office, to inquire if they could do any thing to get me my freedom, and send me back to the West Indies. The gentlemen of the Society took me to a lawyer, who examined very strictly into my case; but told me that the laws of England could do nothing to make me free in Antigua.† However they did all they could for me: they gave me a little money from time to time to keep me from want; and some of them went to Mr. Wood to try to persuade him to let me return a free woman to my husband; but though they offered him, as I have heard, a large sum for my freedom, he was sulky and obstinate, and would not consent to let me go free.

This was the first winter I spent in England, and I suffered much from the severe cold, and from the rheumatic pains, which still at times torment me. However, Providence was very good to me, and I got many friends – especially some Quaker ladies, who hearing of my case, came and sought me out, and gave me good warm clothing and money. Thus I had great cause to bless God in my affliction.

When I got better I was anxious to get some work to do, as I was unwilling to eat the bread of idleness. Mrs. Mash, who was a laundress, recommended me to a lady for a charwoman. She paid me very handsomely for what work I did, and I divided the money with Mrs. Mash; for though very poor, they gave me food when my own money was done, and never suffered me to want.

In the spring, I got into service with a lady, who saw me at the house where I sometimes worked as a

†She came first to the Anti-Slavery Office in Aldermanbury, about the latter end of November 1828; and her case was referred to Mr. George Stephen to be investigated. More of this hereafter. – *Ed.*

charwoman. This lady's name was Mrs. Forsyth. She had been in the West Indies, and was accustomed to Blacks, and liked them. I was with her six months, and went with her to Margate. She treated me well, and gave me a good character when she left London.*

After Mrs. Forsyth went away, I was again out of place, and went to lodgings, for which I paid two shillings a week, and found coals and candle. After eleven weeks, the money I had saved in service was all gone, and I was forced to go back to the Anti-Slavery office to ask a supply, till I could get another situation. I did not like to go back – I did not like to be idle. I would rather work for my living than get it for nothing. They were very good to give me a supply, but I felt shame at being obliged to apply for relief whilst I had strength to work.

At last I went into the service of Mr. and Mrs. Pringle, where I have been ever since, and am as comfortable as I can be while separated from my dear husband, and away from my own country and all old friends and connections. My dear mistress teaches me daily to read the word of God, and takes great pains to make me understand it. I enjoy the great privilege of being enabled to attend church three times on the Sunday; and I have met with many kind friends since I have been here, both clergymen and others. The Rev. Mr. Young, who lives in the next house, has shown me much kindness, and taken much pains to instruct me, particularly while my master and mistress were absent in Scotland. Nor must I forget, among my friends, the Rev. Mr. Mortimer, the good clergyman of the parish, under whose ministry I have now sat for upwards of twelve months. I trust in God I have profited by what I have heard from him. He never keeps back the truth, and I think he has been the means of opening my eyes and ears much better to understand

---

*She refers to a written certificate which will be inserted afterwards.

the word of God. Mr. Mortimer tells me that he cannot open the eyes of my heart, but that I must pray to God to change my heart, and make me to know the truth, and the truth will make me free.

I still live in the hope that God will find a way to give me my liberty, and give me back to my husband. I endeavour to keep down my fretting, and to leave all to Him, for he knows what is good for me better than I know myself. Yet, I must confess, I find it a hard and heavy task to do so.

I am often much vexed, and I feel great sorrow when I hear some people in this country say, that the slaves do not need better usage, and do not want to be free.† They believe the foreign people,‡ who deceive them, and say slaves are happy. I say, Not so. How can slaves be happy when they have the halter round their neck and the whip upon their back? and are disgraced and thought no more of than beasts? – and are separated from their mothers, and husbands, and children, and sisters, just as cattle are sold and separated? Is it happiness for a driver in the field to take down his wife or sister or child, and strip them, and whip them in such a disgraceful manner? – women that have had children exposed in the open field to shame! There is no modesty or decency shown by the owner to his slaves; men, women, and children are exposed alike. Since I have been here I have often wondered how English people can go out into the West Indies and act in such a beastly manner. But when they go to the West Indies, they forget God and all feeling of shame, I think, since they can see and do such things. They tie up slaves like hogs – moor* them up like cattle, and they lick them, so as hogs, or cattle, or horses never

†The whole of this paragraph especially, is given as nearly as was possible in Mary's precise words.
‡She means West Indians.
*A West Indian phrase: to fasten or tie up.

were flogged; – and yet they come home and say, and make some good people believe, that slaves don't want to get out of slavery. But they put a cloak about the truth. It is not so. All slaves want to be free – to be free is very sweet. I will say the truth to English people who may read this history that my good friend, Miss S—, is now writing down for me. I have been a slave myself – I know what slaves feel – I can tell by myself what other slaves feel, and by what they have told me. The man that says slaves be quite happy in slavery – that they don't want to be free – that man is either ignorant or a lying person. I never heard a slave say so. I never heard a Buckra man say so, till I heard tell of it in England. Such people ought to be ashamed of themselves. They can't do without slaves, they say. What's the reason they can't do without slaves as well as in England? No slaves here – no whips – no stocks – no punishment, except for wicked people. They hire servants in England; and if they don't like them, they send them away: they can't lick them. Let them work ever so hard in England, they are far better off than slaves. If they get a bad master, they give warning and go hire to another. They have their liberty. That's just what *we* want. We don't mind hard work, if we had proper treatment, and proper wages like English servants, and proper time given in the week to keep us from breaking the Sabbath. But they won't give it; they will have work – work – work, night and day, sick or well, till we are quite done up; and we must not speak up nor look amiss, however much we be abused. And then when we are quite done up, who cares for us, more than for a lame horse? This is slavery. I tell it to let English people know the truth; and I hope they will never leave off to pray God, and call loud to the great King of England, till all the poor blacks be given free, and slavery done up for evermore.

Supplement to the
History of Mary Prince

By *the Original Editor, Thomas Pringle*

Leaving Mary's narrative, for the present, without comment to the reader's reflections, I proceed to state some circumstances connected with her case which have fallen more particularly under my own notice, and which I consider it incumbent now to lay fully before the public.

About the latter end of November, 1828, this poor woman found her way to the office of the Anti-Slavery Society in Aldermanbury, by the aid of a person who had become acquainted with her situation, and had advised her to apply there for advice and assistance. After some preliminary examination into the accuracy of the circumstances related by her, I went along with her to Mr. George Stephen, solicitor, and requested him to investigate and draw up a statement of her case, and have it submitted to counsel, in order to ascertain whether or not, under the circumstances, her freedom could be legally established on her return to Antigua. On this occasion, in Mr. Stephen's presence and mine, she expressed, in very strong terms, her anxiety to return thither if she could go as a free person, and, at the same time, her extreme apprehensions of the fate that would probably await her if she returned as a slave. Her words were, 'I would rather go into my grave than go back a slave to Antigua, though I wish to go back to my husband very much – very much – very much! I am much afraid my owners would separate me from my husband, and use me very hard, or perhaps sell me for a field negro; – and slavery is too too bad. I would rather go into my grave!'

The paper which Mr. Wood had given her before she left his house, was placed by her in Mr. Stephen's hands. It was expressed in the following terms:-

'I have already told Molly, and now give it her in writing, in order that there may be no misunderstanding on her part, that as I brought her from Antigua at her own request and entreaty, and that she is consequently now free, she is of course at liberty to take her baggage and go where she pleases. And, in consequence of her late conduct, she must do one of two things – either quit the house, or return to Antigua by the earliest opportunity, as she does not evince a disposition to make herself useful. As she is a stranger in London, I do not wish to turn her out, or would do so, as two female servants are sufficient for my establishment. If after this she does remain, it will be only during her good behaviour; but on no considera-tion will I allow her wages or any other remuneration for her services.

'JOHN A. WOOD'
'London, August 18, 1828.'

This paper, though not devoid of inconsistencies, which will be apparent to any attentive reader, is craftily expressed; and was well devised to serve the purpose which the writer had obviously in view, namely, to frustrate any appeal which the friendless black woman might make to the sympathy of strangers, and thus prevent her from obtaining an asylum, if she left his house, from any respectable family. As she had no one to refer to for a character in this country except himself, he doubtless calculated securely on her being speedily driven back, as soon as the slender fund she had in her possession was expended, to throw herself unconditionally upon his tender mercies; and his disappointment in this expectation appears to have exasperated his feelings of resentment towards the poor woman, to a degree which few persons alive to the claims of common justice, not to speak of christianity or common humanity, could easily have anticipated. Such, at least, seems the only intelligible inference that can be drawn from his subsequent conduct.

The case having been submitted, by desire of the Anti-Slavery Committee, to the consideration of Dr. Lushington and Mr. Sergeant Stephen, it was found that there existed no legal means of compelling Mary's master to grant her manumission; and that if she returned to Antigua, she would inevitably fall again under his power, or that of his attorneys, as a slave. It was, however, resolved to try what could be effected for her by amicable negotiation; and with this view Mr. Ravenscroft, a solicitor, (Mr. Stephen's relative,) called upon Mr. Wood, in order to ascertain whether he would consent to Mary's manumission on any reasonable terms, and to refer, if required, the amount of compensation for her value to arbitration. Mr. Ravenscroft with some difficulty obtained one or two interviews, but found Mr. Wood so full of animosity against the woman, and so firmly bent against any arrangement having her freedom for its object, that the negotiation was soon broken off as hopeless. The angry slave-owner declared 'that he would not move a finger about her in this country, or grant her manumission on any terms whatever; and that if she went back to the West Indies, she must take the consequences.'

This unreasonable conduct of Mr. Wood, induced the Anti-Slavery Committee, after several other abortive attempts to effect a compromise, to think of bringing the case under the notice of Parliament. The heads of Mary's statement were accordingly engrossed in a Petition, which

Dr. Lushington offered to present, and to give notice at the same time of his intention to bring in a Bill to provide for the entire emancipation of all slaves brought to England with the owner's consent. But before this step was taken, Dr. Lushington again had recourse to negociation with the master; and, partly through the friendly intervention of Mr. Manning, partly by personal conference, used every persuasion in his power to induce Mr. Wood to relent and let the bondwoman go free. Seeing the matter thus seriously taken up, Mr. Wood became at length alarmed, – not relishing, it appears, the idea of having the case publicly discussed in the House of Commons; and to avert this result he submitted to temporize – assumed a demeanour of unwonted civility, and even hinted to Mr. Manning (as I was given to understand) that if he was not driven to utter hostility by the threatened exposure, he would probably meet our wishes 'in his own time and way.' Having gained time by these manœuvres, he adroitly endeavoured to cool the ardour of Mary's new friends, in her cause, by representing her as an abandoned and worthless woman, ungrateful towards him, and undeserving of sympathy from others; allegations which he supported by the ready affirmation of some of his West India friends, and by one or two plausible letters procured from Antigua. By these and like artifices he appears completely to have imposed on Mr. Manning, the respectable West India merchant whom Dr. Lushington had asked to negotiate with him; and he prevailed so far as to induce Dr. Lushington himself (actuated by the benevolent view of thereby best serving Mary's cause,) to abstain from any remarks upon his conduct when the petition was at last presented in Parliament. In this way he dextrously contrived to neutralize all our efforts, until the close of the Session of 1829; soon after which he embarked with his family for the West Indies.

Every exertion for Mary's relief having thus failed; and being fully convinced from a twelvemonth's observation of her conduct, that she was really a well-disposed and respectable woman; I engaged her, in December 1829, as a domestic servant in my own family. In this capacity she has remained ever since; and I am thus enabled to speak of her conduct and character with a degree of confidence I could not have otherwise done. The importance of this circumstance will appear in the sequel.

From the time of Mr. Wood's departure to Antigua, in 1829, till June or July last, no farther effort was attempted for Mary's relief. Some faint hope was still cherished that this unconscionable man would at length relent, and 'in his own time and way,' grant the prayer of the exiled negro woman. After waiting, however, nearly twelvemonths and longer, and seeing the poor woman's spirits daily sinking under the sickening influence of hope deferred, I resolved on a final attempt in her behalf, through the intervention of the Moravian Missionaries, and of the Governor of Antigua. At my request, Mr. Edward Moore, agent of the Moravian Brethren in London, wrote to the Rev. Joseph Newby, their Missionary in that island, empowering him to negotiate in his own name with Mr. Wood for Mary's manumission, and to procure his consent, if possible, upon terms of ample pecuniary compensation. At the same time the excellent and benevolent William Allen, of the Society of Friends, wrote to Sir Patrick Ross, the Governor of the Colony, with whom he was on terms of friendship, soliciting him to use his influence in persuading Mr. Wood to consent; and I confess I was sanguine enough to flatter myself that we should thus at length prevail. The result proved, however, that I had not yet fully appreciated the character of the man we had to deal with.

Mr. Newby's answer arrived early in November last, mentioning that he had done all in his power to accomplish our purpose, but in vain; and that if Mary's manumission could not be obtained without Mr. Wood's consent, he believed there was no prospect of its ever being effected.

A few weeks afterwards I was informed by Mr. Allen, that he had received a letter from Sir Patrick Ross, stating that he also had used his best endeavours in the affair, but equally without effect. Sir Patrick at the same time inclosed a letter, addressed by Mr. Wood to his Secretary, Mr. Taylor, assigning his reasons for persisting in this extraordinary course. This letter requires our special attention. Its tenor is as follows:-

'My dear Sir,

'In reply to your note relative to the woman Molly, I beg you will have the kindness to oblige me by assuring his Excellency that I regret exceedingly my inability to comply with his request, which under other circumstances would afford me very great pleasure.

'There are many and powerful reasons for inducing me to refuse my sanction to her returning here in the way she seems to wish. It would be to reward the worst species of ingratitude, and subject myself to insult whenever she came in my way. Her moral character is very bad, as the police records will shew; and she would be a very troublesome character should she come here without any restraint. She is not a native of this country, and I know of no relation she has here. I induced her to take a husband, a short time before she left this, by providing a comfortable house in my yard for them, and prohibiting her going out after 10 to 12 o'clock (our bed-time) without special leave. This she considered the greatest, and indeed the only, grievance she ever complained of, and all my efforts could not prevent it. In hopes of inducing her to be steady to her husband, who was a free man, I gave him the house to occupy during our absence; but it appears the attachment was too loose to bind her, and he has taken another wife; so on that score I do her no injury. – In England she made her election and quitted my family. This I had no right to object to; and I should have thought no more of it, but not satisfied to leave quietly, she gave every trouble and annoyance in her power, and endeavoured to injure the character of my family by the most vile and infamous falsehoods, which was embodied in a petition to the House of Commons, and would have been presented, had not my friends from this island, particularly the Hon. Mr. Byam and Dr. Coull, come forward, and disproved what she had asserted.

'It would be beyond the limits of an ordinary letter to detail her baseness, though I will do so should his Excellency wish it; but you may judge of her depravity by one circumstance, which came out before Mr. Justice Dyett, in a quarrel with another female.

* * *

'Such a thing I could not have believed possible.*

'Losing her value as a slave in a pecuniary point of view I consider of no consequence; for it was our intention, had she conducted herself properly and returned with us, to have given her freedom. She has taken her freedom; and all I wish is, that she would enjoy it without meddling with me.

'Let me again repeat, if his Excellency wishes it, it will afford me great pleasure to state such particulars of her, and which will be incontestably proved by

---

*I omit the circumstance here mentioned, because it is too indecent to appear in a publication likely to be perused by females. It is, in all probability, a vile calumny; but even if it were perfectly true, it would not serve Mr. Wood's case one straw. – Any reader who wishes it, may see the passage referred to, in the autograph letter in my possession. T.P.

numbers here, that I am sure will acquit me in his opinion of acting unkind or ungenerous towards her. I'll say nothing of the liability I should incur, under the Consolidated Slave Law, of dealing with a free person as a slave.

'My only excuse for entering so much into detail must be that of my anxious wish to stand justified in his Excellency's opinion.

'I am, my dear Sir,
    Yours very truly,
        JOHN A. WOOD.
            '20*th* Oct. 1830.'
'Charles Taylor, Esq.
    &c. &c. &c.

'I forgot to mention that it was at her own special request that she accompanied me to England – and also that she had a considerable sum of money with her, which she had saved in my service. I knew of £36 or £40, at least, for I had some trouble to recover it from a white man, to whom she had lent it.

'J.A.W.'

Such is Mr. Wood's justification of his conduct in thus obstinately refusing manumission to the Negro-woman who had escaped from his 'house-of-bondage.'

Let us now endeavour to estimate the validity of the excuses assigned, and the allegations advanced by him, for the information of Governor Sir Patrick Ross, in this deliberate statement of his case.

1. To allow the woman to return home free, would, he affirms 'be to reward the worst species of ingratitude.'

He assumes, it seems, the sovereign power of pronouncing a virtual sentence of banishment, for the alleged crime of ingratitude. Is this then a power which any man ought to possess over his fellow-mortal? or which any good man would ever wish to exercise? And, besides, there is no evidence whatever, beyond Mr. Wood's mere assertion, that Mary Prince owed him or his family the slightest mark of gratitude. Her account of the treatment she received in his service, *may* be incorrect; but her simple statement is at least supported by minute and feasible details, and, unless rebutted by positive facts, will certainly command credence from impartial minds more readily than his angry accusation, which has something absurd and improbable in its very front. Moreover, is it not absurd to term the assertion of her *natural rights* by a slave, – even supposing her to have been kindly dealt with by her 'owners,' and treated in every respect the reverse of what Mary affirms to have been her treatment by Mr. Wood and his wife, – 'the *worst* species of ingratitude?' This may be West Indian ethics, but it will scarcely be received as sound doctrine in Europe.

2. To permit her return would be 'to subject himself to insult whenever she came in his way.'

This is a most extraordinary assertion. Are the laws of Antigua then so favourable to the free blacks, or the colonial police so feebly administered, that there are no sufficient restraints to protect a rich colonist like Mr. Wood, – a man who counts among his familiar friends the Honourable Mr. Byam, and Mr. Taylor the Government Secretary, – from being insulted by a poor Negro-woman? It is preposterous.

3. Her moral character is so bad, that she would prove very troublesome should she come to the colony 'without any restraint.'

'Any restraint?' Are there no restraints (supposing them necessary) short of absolute slavery to keep 'troublesome characters' in order? But this, I suppose, is the *argumentum ad gubernatorem* – to frighten the governor. She is such a termagant, it seems, that if she once gets back to the colony *free*, she will not only make it too hot for poor Mr. Wood, but the police and courts of justice will scarce be a match for her! Sir Patrick Ross, no doubt, will take care how he intercedes farther for so formidable a virago! How can one treat such arguments seriously?

4. She is not a native of the colony, and he knows of no relation she has there.

True: But was it not her home (so far as a slave can have a home) for thirteen or fourteen years? Were not the connexions, friendships, and associations of her mature life formed there? Was it not there she hoped to spend her latter years in domestic tranquillity with her husband, free from the lash of the taskmaster? These considerations may appear light to Mr. Wood, but they are every thing to this poor woman.

5. He induced her, he says, to take a husband, a short time before she left Antigua, and gave them a comfortable house in his yard, &c. &c.

This paragraph merits attention. He '*induced her to take a husband?*' If the fact were true, what brutality of mind and manners does it not indicate among these slave-holders? They refuse to legalize the marriages of their slaves, but *induce* them to form such temporary connexions as may suit the owner's conveniency, just as they would pair the lower animals; and this man has the effrontery to tell us so! Mary, however, tells a very different story, (see page 74;) and her assertion, independently of other proof, is at least as credible as Mr. Wood's. The reader will judge for himself as to the preponderance of internal evidence in the conflicting statements.

6. He alleges that she was, before marriage, licentious,

and even depraved in her conduct, and unfaithful to her husband afterwards.

These are serious charges. But if true, or even partially true, how comes it that a person so correct in his family hours and arrangements as Mr. Wood professes to be, and who expresses so edifying a horror of licentiousness, could reconcile it to his conscience to keep in the bosom of his family so *depraved*, as well as so *troublesome* a character for at least thirteen years, and confide to her for long periods too the charge of his house and the care of his children – for such I shall shew to have been the facts? How can he account for not having rid himself with all speed, of so disreputable an inmate – he who values her loss so little 'in a pecuniary point of view?' How can he account for having sold *five other slaves* in that period, and yet have retained this shocking woman – nay, even have refused to sell her, on more than one occasion, when offered her full value? It could not be from ignorance of her character, for the circumstance which he adduces as a proof of her shameless depravity, and which I have omitted on account of its indecency, occurred, it would appear, not less than *ten years ago*. Yet, notwithstanding her alleged ill qualities and habits of gross immorality, he has not only constantly refused to part with her; but after thirteen long years, brings her to England as an attendant on his wife and children, with the avowed intention of carrying her back along with his maiden daughter, a young lady returning from school! Such are the extra-ordinary facts; and until Mr. Wood shall reconcile these singular inconsistencies between his actions and his allegations, he must not be surprised if we in England prefer giving credit to the former rather than the latter; although at present it appears somewhat difficult to say which side of the alternative is the more creditable to his own character.

7. Her husband, he says, has taken another wife; 'so that on that score,' he adds, 'he does her no injury.'

Supposing this fact be true, (which I doubt, as I doubt every mere assertion from so questionable a quarter,) I shall take leave to put a question or two to Mr. Wood's conscience. Did he not write from England to his friend Mr. Darrel, soon after Mary left his house, directing him to turn her husband, Daniel James, off his premises, on account of her offence; telling him to inform James at the same time that his wife had *taken up* with another man, who had robbed her of all she had – a calumny as groundless as it was cruel? I further ask if the person who invented this story (whoever he may be,) was not likely enough to impose similar fabrications on the poor negro man's credulity, until he may have been induced to prove false to his marriage vows, and to 'take another wife,' as Mr. Wood coolly expresses it? but withal, I strongly doubt the fact of Daniel James' infidelity; for there is now before me a letter from himself to Mary, dated in April 1830, couched in strong terms of conjugal affection; expressing his anxiety for her speedy return, and stating that he had lately 'received a grace' (a token of religious advancement) in the Moravian church, a circumstance altogether incredible if the man were living in open adultery, as Mr. Wood's assertion implies.

8. Mary, he says, endeavoured to injure the character of his family by infamous falsehoods, which were embodied in a petition to the House of Commons, and would have been presented, had not his friends from Antigua, the Hon. Mr. Byam, and Dr. Coull, disproved her assertions.

I can say something on this point from my own knowledge. Mary's petition contained simply a brief statement of her case, and, among other things, mentioned the treatment she had received from Mr. and Mrs. Wood. Now the principal facts are corroborated by other evidence, and Mr. Wood must bring forward very different testimony from that of Dr. Coull before well-informed persons will give credit to his contradiction. The value of that person's evidence in such cases will be noticed presently. Of the Hon. Mr. Byam I know nothing, and shall only at present remark that it is not likely to redound greatly to his credit to appear in such company. Futhermore, Mary's petition *was* presented, as Mr. Wood ought to know; though it was not discussed, nor his conduct exposed as it ought to have been.

9. He speaks of the liability he should incur, under the Consolidated Slave Law, of dealing with a free person as a slave.

Is not this pretext hypocritical in the extreme? What liability could he possibly incur by voluntarily resigning the power, conferred on him by an iniquitous colonial law, of re-imposing the shackles of slavery on the bondwoman from whose limbs they had fallen when she touched the free soil of England? – There exists no liability from which he might not have been easily secured, or for which he would not have been fully compensated.

He adds in a postscript that Mary had a considerable sum of money with her, – from £36 to £40 at least, which she had saved in his service. The fact is, that she had at one time 113 dollars in cash; but only a very small portion of that sum appears to have been brought by her to England, the rest having been partly advanced, as she states, to assist her husband, and partly lost by being lodged in unfaithful custody.

Finally, Mr. Wood repeats twice that it will afford him great pleasure to state for the governor's satisfaction, if required, such particulars of 'the woman Molly,' upon incontestable evidence, as he is sure will acquit him in his Excellency's opinion 'of acting unkind or ungenerous towards her.'

This is well: and I now call upon Mr. Wood to redeem his pledge; – to bring forward facts and proofs fully to elucidate the subject; – to reconcile, if he can, the extraordinary discrepancies which I have pointed out between his assertions and the actual facts, and especially between his account of Mary Prince's character and his own conduct in regard to her. He has now to produce such a statement as will acquit him not only in the opinion of Sir Patrick Ross, but of the British public. And in this position he has spontaneously placed himself, in attempting to destroy, by his deliberate criminatory letter, the poor woman's fair fame and reputation, – an attempt but for which the present publication would probably never have appeared.

Here perhaps we might safely leave the case to the judgment of the public; but as this negro woman's character, not the less valuable to her because her condition is so humble, has been so unscrupulously blackened by her late master, a party so much interested and inclined to place her in the worst point of view, – it is incumbent on me, as her advocate with the public, to state such additional testimony in her behalf as I can fairly and conscientiously adduce.

My first evidence is Mr. Joseph Phillips, of Antigua. Having submitted to his inspection Mr. Wood's letter and Mary Prince's narrative, and requested his candid and deliberate sentiments in regard to the actual facts of the case, I have been favoured with the following letter from him on the subject:-

'London, January 18, 1831.

'Dear Sir,

'In giving you my opinion of Mary Prince's narrative, and of Mr. Wood's letter respecting her, addressed to Mr. Taylor, I shall first mention my opportunities of forming a proper estimate of the conduct and character of both parties.

'I have known Mr. Wood since his first arrival in Antigua in 1803. He was then a poor young man, who had been brought up as a ship carpenter in Bermuda. He was afterwards raised to be a clerk in the Commissariat department, and realised sufficient capital to commence business as a merchant. This last profession he has followed successfully for a good many years, and is understood to have accumulated very considerable wealth. After he entered into trade, I had constant intercourse with him in the way of business; and in 1824 and 1825, I was regularly employed on his premises as his clerk; consequently, I had opportunities of seeing a good deal of his character both as a merchant and as a master of slaves. The former topic I pass over as irrelevant to the present subject: in reference to the latter, I shall merely observe that he was not, in regard to ordinary matters, more severe than the ordinary run of slave owners; but, if seriously offended, he was not of a disposition to be easily appeased, and would spare no cost or sacrifice to gratify his vindictive feelings. As regards the exaction of work from domestic slaves, his wife was probably more severe than himself – it was almost impossible for the slaves ever to give her entire satisfaction.

'Of their slave Molly (or Mary) I know less than of Mr. and Mrs. Wood; but I saw and heard enough of her, both while I was constantly employed on Mr. Wood's premises, and while I was there occasionally on business, to be quite cetain that she was viewed by her owners as their most respectable and trustworthy female slave. It is within my personal knowledge that she had usually the charge of the house in their absence, was entrusted with the keys, &c.; and was always considered by the neighbours and visitors as their confidential household servant, and as a person in whose integrity they placed unlimited confidence, – although when Mrs. Wood was at home, she was no doubt kept pretty closely at washing and other hard work. A decided proof of the estimation in which she was held by her owners exists in the fact that Mr. Wood uniformly refused to part with her, whereas he sold five other slaves while she was with them. Indeed, she always appeared to me to be a slave of superior intelligence and respectability; and I always understood such to be her general character in the place.

'As to what Mr. Wood alleges about her being frequently before the police, &c. I can only say I never heard of the circumstance before; and as I lived for twenty years in the same small town, and in the vicinity of their residence, I think I could scarcely have failed to become acquainted with it, had such been the fact. She might, however, have been occasionally before the magistrate in consequence of little disputes among the slaves, without any serious imputation on her general respectability. She says she was twice summoned to appear as a witness on such occasions; and that she was once sent by her mistress to be confined in the Cage, and was afterwards flogged by her desire. This cruel practice is very common in Antigua; and, in my opinion, is but little creditable to the slave owners and magistrates by whom such arbitrary punishments are inflicted, frequently for very trifling faults. Mr. James Scotland is the only magistrate in the colony who invariably refuses to sanction this reprehensible practice.

'Of the immoral conduct ascribed to Molly by Mr. Wood, I can say nothing further than this – that I have heard she had at a former period (previous to her marriage) a connexion with a white person, a Capt.—, which I have no doubt was broken off when she became seriously impressed with religion. But, at any rate, such connexions are so common, I might almost say universal, in our slave colonies, that except by the missionaries and a few serious persons, they are considered, if faults at all, so very venial as scarcely to deserve the name of immorality. Mr. Wood knows this colonial estimate of such connexions as well as I do; and, however false such an estimate must be allowed to be, especially when applied to their own conduct by persons of education, pretending to adhere to the pure Christian rule of morals, – yet when he ascribes to a negro slave, to whom legal marriage was denied, such great criminality for laxity of this sort, and professes to be so exceedingly shocked and amazed at the tale he himself relates, he must, I am confident, have had a farther object in view than the information of Mr. Taylor or Sir Patrick Ross. He must, it is evident, have been aware that his letter would be sent to Mr. Allen, and accordingly adapted it, as more important documents from the colonies are often adapted, *for effect in England*. The tale of the slave Molly's immoralities, be assured, was not intended for Antigua so much as for Stoke Newington, and Peckham, and Aldermanbury.

'In regard to Mary's narrative generally, although I cannot speak to the accuracy of the details, except in a few recent particulars, I can with safety declare that I see no reason to question the truth of a single fact stated by her, or even to suspect her in any instance of intentional exaggeration. It bears in my judgment the genuine stamp of truth and nature. Such is my unhesitating opinion, after a residence of twenty-seven years in the West Indies.

'I remain, &c.

'JOSPEPH PHILLIPS.'

'*P.S.* As Mr. Wood refers to the evidence of Dr. T. Coull in opposition to Mary's assertions, it may be proper to enable you justly to estimate the worth of that person's evidence in cases connected with the condition and treatment of slaves. You are aware that in 1829, Mr. McQueen of Glasgow, in noticing a Report of the "Ladies' Society of Birmingham for the relief of British Negro Slaves," asserted with his characteristic audacity, that the statement which it contained respecting distressed and deserted slaves in Antigua was "an abominable falsehood." Not contented with this, and with insinuating that I, as agent of the society in the distribution of their charity in Antigua, had fraudulently duped them out of their money by a fabricated tale of distress, Mr. McQueen proceeded to libel me in the most opprobrious terms, as "a man of the most worthless and abandoned character."* Now I know from good authority that it

*In elucidation of the circumstances above referred to, I subjoin the following extracts from the Report by the Birmingham Ladies' Society for 1830:-

'As a portion of the funds of this association has been appropriated to assist the benevolent efforts of a society which has for fifteen years afforded relief to distressed and deserted slaves in Antigua, it may not be uninteresting to our friends to learn the manner in which the agent of this society has been treated for simply obeying the command of our Saviour, by ministering, like the good Samaritan, to the distresses of the helpless and the desolate. The society's proceedings being adverted to by a friend of Africa, at one of the public meetings held in this country, a West Indian planter, who was present, wrote over to his friends in Antigua, and represented the conduct of the distributors of this charity in such a light, that it was deemed worthy of the cognizance of the House of Assembly. Mr. Joseph Phillips, a resident of the island, who had most kindly and disinterestedly exerted himself in the distribution of the money from England among the poor deserted slaves, was brought before the Assembly, and most severely interrogated: on his refusing to deliver up his private correspondence with his friends in England, he was thrown into a loathsome jail, where he was kept for nearly five months; while his loss of was *upon Dr. Coull's information* that Mr. McQueen founded this impudent contradiction of notorious facts, and this audacious libel of my personal character. From this single circumstance you may judge of the value of his evidence in the case of Mary Prince. I can furnish further information respecting Dr. Coull's colonial

---

business, and the oppressive proceeding instituted against him, were involving him in poverty and ruin. On his discharge by the House of Assembly, he was seized in their lobby for debt, and again imprisoned.'

'In our report for the year 1826, we quoted a passage from the 13th Report of the Society for the relief of deserted Slaves in the island of Antigua, in reference to a case of great distress. This statement fell into the hands of Mr. McQueen, the Editor of the Glasgow Courier. Of the consequences resulting from this circumstance we only gained information through the Leicester Chronicle, which had copied an article from the Weekly Register of Antigua, dated St. John's, September 22, 1829. We find from this that Mr. McQueen affirms, that "with the exception of the fact that the society is, as it deserves to be, duped out of its money, the whole tale" (of the distress above referred to) "is an abominable falsehood." This statement, which we are informed has appeared in many of the public papers, is COMPLETELY REFUTED in our Appendix No. 4, to which we refer our readers. Mr. McQueen's statements, we regret to say, would lead many to believe that there are no deserted Negroes to assist; and that the case mentioned was a perfect fabrication. He also distinctly avers, that the disinterested and humane agent of the society, Mr. Joseph Phillips, is "a man of the most worthless and abandoned character." In opposition to this statement, we learn the good character of Mr. Phillips from those who have long been acquainted with his laudable exertions in the cause of humanity, . . ." from the Editor of the Weekly Register of Antigua, who speaks, on his own knowledge, of more than twenty years back; confidently appealing at the same time to the inhabitants of the colony in which he resides for the truth of his averments, and producing a testimonial to Mr. Phillips's good character signed by two members of the Antigua House of Assembly, and by Mr. Wyke, the collector of his Majesty's customs, and by Antigua merchants, as follows – "that they have been acquainted with him the last four years and upwards, and he has always conducted himself in an upright becoming manner – his character we know to be unimpeached, and his morals unexceptionable."

Signed 'Thomas Saunderson John D. Taylor
John A. Wood George Wyke
Samuel L. Darrel Giles S.Musson
Robert Grant.'
St. John's, Antigua, June 28, 1825.'

In addition to the above testimonies, Mr. Phillips has brought over to England with him others of a more recent date, from some of the most respectable persons in Antigua – sufficient to cover with confusion all his unprincipled calumniators. See also his account of his own case in the Anti-Slavery Reporter, No. 74, p. 69.

proceedings, both private and judicial, should circumstances require it.'

'J.P.'

I leave the preceding letter to be candidly weighed by the reader in opposition to the inculpatory allegations of Mr. Wood – merely remarking that Mr. Wood will find it somewhat difficult to impugn the evidence of Mr. Phillips, whose 'upright,' 'unimpeached,' and 'unexceptionable' character, he has himself vouched for in unqualified terms, by affixing his signature to the testimonial published in the Weekly Register of Antigua in 1825. (See Note below.)

The next testimony in Mary's behalf is that of Mrs. Forsyth, a lady in whose service she spent the summer of 1829. – (See page 81.) This lady, on leaving London to join her husband, voluntarily presented Mary with a certificate, which, though it relates only to a recent and short period of her history, is a strong corroboration of the habitual respectability of her character. It is in the following terms:-

'Mrs. Forsyth states, that the bearer of this paper (Mary James,) has been with her for the last six months; that she has found her an excellent character, being honest, industrious, and sober; and that she parts with her on no other account than this – that being obliged to travel with her husband, who has lately come from abroad in bad health, she has no farther need of a servant. Any person wishing to engage her, can have her character in full from Miss Robson, 4, Keppel Street, Russel Square, whom Mrs. Forsyth has requested to furnish particulars to any one desiring them.

'4, Keppel Street, 28th Sept. 1829.'

In the last place, I add my own testimony in behalf of this negro woman. Independently of the scrutiny, which, as Secretary of the Anti-Slavery Society, I made into her case when she first applied for assistance, at 18, Aldermanbury, and the watchful eye I kept upon her conduct for the ensuing twelvemonths, while she was the occasional pensioner of the Society, I have now had the opportunity of closely observing her conduct for fourteen months, in the situation of a domestic servant in my own family; and the following is the deliberate opinion of Mary's character, formed not only by myself, but also by my wife and sister-in-law, after this ample period of observation. We have found her perfectly honest and trustworthy in all respects; so that we have no hestitation in leaving every thing in the house at her disposal. She had the entire charge of the house during our absence in Scotland for three months last autumn, and conducted herself in that charge with the utmost discretion and fidelity. She is not, it is true, a very expert housemaid, nor capable of much hard work, (for her constitution appears to be a good deal broken,) but she is careful, industrious, and anxious to do her duty and to give satisfaction. She is capable of strong attachments, and feels deep, though unobtrusive, gratitude for real kindness shown her. She possesses considerable natural sense, and has much quickness of observation and discrimination of character. She is remarkable for *decency* and *propriety* of conduct – and her *delicacy*, even in trifling minutiæ, has been a trait of special remark by the females of my family. This trait, which is obviously quite unaffected, would be a most inexplicable anomaly, if her former habits had been so indecent and depraved as Mr. Wood alleges. Her chief faults, so far as we have discovered them, are, a somewhat violent and hasty temper, and a considerable share of natural pride and self-importance; but these defects have been but rarely and transiently manifested, and have scarcely occasioned an hour's uneasiness at any time in our household. Her religious knowledge, notwithstanding the pious care of her Moravian instructors in Antigua, is still but very limited, and her views of christianity indistinct; but her profession, whatever it may have of imperfection, I am convinced, has nothing of insincerity. In short, we consider her on the whole as respectable and well-behaved a person in her station, as any domestic, white or black, (and we have had ample experience of both colours,) that we have ever had in our service.

But after all, Mary's character, important though its exculpation be to her, is not really the point of chief practical interest in this case. Suppose all Mr. Wood's defamatory allegations to be true – suppose him to be able to rake up against her out of the records of the Antigua police, or from the veracious testimony of his brother colonists, twenty stories as bad or worse than what he insinuates – suppose the whole of her own statement to be false, and even the whole of her conduct since she came under our observation here to be a tissue of hypocrisy; – suppose all this – and leave the negro woman as black in character as in complexion,* – yet it would affect not the main facts – which are these. – 1. Mr. Wood, not daring in England to punish this woman arbitrarily, as he would have done in the West Indies, drove her out of his house, or left her, at least, only the alternative of returning instantly to Antigua, with the certainty of severe treatment there, or submitting in

---

*If it even were so, how strong a plea of palliation might not the poor negro bring, by adducing the neglect of her various owners to afford religious instruction or moral discipline, and the habitual influence of their evil *example* (to say the very least,) before her eyes? What moral good could she possibly learn – what moral evil could she easily escape, while under the uncontrolled power of such masters as she describes Captain I— and Mr. D— of Turk's Island? All things considered, it is indeed wonderful to find her such as she now is. But as she herself piously expressed it, 'that God whom then she knew not mercifully preserved her for better things.'

silence to what she considered intolerable usage in his household. 2. He has since obstinately persisted in refusing her manumission, to enable her to return home in security, though repeatedly offered more than ample compensation for her value as a slave; and this on various frivolous pretexts, but really, and indeed not unavowedly, in order to *punish* her for leaving his service in England, though he himself had professed to give her that option. These unquestionable facts speak volumes.*

*Since the preceding pages were printed off, I have been favoured with a communication from the Rev. J. Curtin, to whom among other acquaintances of Mr. Wood's in this country, the entire proof sheets of this pamphlet had been sent for inspection. Mr. Curtin corrects some omissions and inaccuracies in Mary Prince's narrative (see page 74,) by stating, 1. That she was baptized, not in August, but on the 6th April, 1817; 2. That sometime before her baptism, on her being admitted a catechumen, preparatory to that holy ordinance, she brought a note from her owner, Mr. Wood, recommending her for religious instruction, &c.; 3. That it was his usual practice, when any adult slaves came on *week days* to school, to require their owner's permission for their attendance; but that on *Sundays* the chapel was open indiscriminately to all. – Mary, after a personal interview with Mr. Curtin, and after hearing his letter read by me, still maintains that Mr. Wood's note recommended her for baptism merely, and that she never received any religious instruction whatever from Mr. and Mrs. Wood, or from any one else at that period beyond what she has stated in her narrative. In regard to her non-admission to the Sunday school without permission from her owners, she admits that she may possibly have mistaken the clergyman's meaning on that point, but says that such was certainly her impression at the time, and the actual cause of her non-attendance.

Mr. Curtin finds in his books some reference to Mary's connection with a Captain —, (the individual, I believe, alluded to by Mr. Phillips at page 101); but he states that when she attended his chapel she was always decently and becomingly dressed, and appeared to him to be in a situation of trust in her mistress's family.

Mr. Curtin offers no comment on any other part of Mary's statement; but he speaks in very favourable, though general terms of the respectability of Mr. Wood, whom he had known for many years in Antigua; and of Mrs. Wood, though she was not personally known to him, he says, that he had 'heard her spoken of by those of her acquaintance, as a lady of very mild and amiable manners.'

Another friend of Mr. and Mrs. Wood, a lady who had been their guest both in Antigua and England, alleges that Mary has grossly misrepresented them in her narrative; she says that she 'can vouch for their being the most benevolent, kind-hearted people that can possibly live.' She has declined, however, to furnish me with any written correction of the misrepresentations she complains of, although I offered to insert her testimony in behalf of her friends, if sent to me in time. And having already kept back the publication a fortnight waiting for communications of this sort, I will not delay it longer. Those who have withheld their strictures have only themselves to blame.

The case affords a most instructive illustration of the true spirit of the slave system, and of the pretensions of the slaveholders to assert, not merely their claims to a 'vested right' in the *labour* of their bondmen, but to an indefeasible property in them as their 'absolute chattels.' It furnishes a striking practical comment on the assertions of the West Indians that self-interest is a sufficient check to the indulgence of vindictive feelings in the master; for here is a case where a man (a *respectable* and *benevolent* man as his friends aver,) prefers losing entirely the full price of the slave, for the mere satisfaction of preventing a poor black woman from returning home to her husband! If the pleasure of thwarting the benevolent wishes of the Anti-Slavery Society in behalf of the deserted negro, be an additional motive with Mr. Wood, it will not much mend his wretched plea.

I may here add a few words respecting the earlier portion of Mary Prince's narrative. The facts there stated must necessarily rest entirely, – since we have no collateral evidence, – upon their intrinsic claims to probability, and upon the reliance the reader may feel disposed, after perusing the foregoing pages, to place on her veracity. To my judgment, the internal evidence of the truth of her

---

Of the general character of Mr. and Mrs. Wood, I would not designedly give any *unfair* impression. Without implicitly adopting either the *ex parte* view of Mary Prince, or the unmeasured encomiums of their friends, I am willing to believe them to be, on the whole, fair, perhaps favourable, specimens of colonial character. Let them even be rated, if you will, in the very highest and most benevolent class of slaveholders; and, laying every thing else entirely out of view, let Mr. Wood's conduct in this affair be tried exclusively by the facts established beyond dispute, and by his own statement of the case in his letter to Mr. Taylor. But then, I ask, if the very *best* and *mildest* of your slave-owners can act as Mr. Wood is proved to have acted, what is to be expected of persons whose mildness, or equity, or common humanity no one will dare to vouch for? If such things are done in the green tree, what will be done in the dry? – And what else can Colonial Slavery possibly be, even in its best estate, but a system incurably evil and iniquitous? – I require no other data – I need add no further comment.

narrative appears remarkably strong. The circumstances are related in a tone of natural sincerity, and are accompanied in almost every case with characteristic and minute details, which must, I conceive, carry with them full conviction to every candid mind that this negro woman has actually seen, felt, and suffered all that she so impressively describes; and that the picture she has given of West Indian slavery is not less true than it is revolting.

But there may be some persons into whose hands this tract may fall, so imperfectly acquainted with the real character of Negro Slavery, as to be shocked into partial, if not absolute incredulity, by the acts of inhuman oppression and brutality related of Capt. I— and his wife, and of Mr. D—, the salt manufacturer of Turk's Island. Here, at least, such persons may be disposed to think, there surely must be *some* exaggeration; the facts are too shocking to be credible. The facts are indeed shocking, but unhappily not the less credible on that account. Slavery is a curse to the oppressor scarcely less than to the oppressed: its natural tendency is to brutalize both. After a residence myself of six years in a slave colony, I am inclined to doubt whether, as regards its *demoralizing* influence, the master is not even a greater object of compassion than his bondman. Let those who are disposed to doubt the atrocities related in this narrative, on the testimony of a sufferer, examine the details of many cases of similar barbarity that have lately come before the public, on unquestionable evidence. Passing over the reports of the Fiscal of Berbice,* and the Mauritius horrors recently unveiled,† let them consider the case of Mr. and Mrs. Moss, of the Bahamas, and their slave Kate, so justly denounced by the Secretary for the Colonies;‡ – the cases of Eleanor Mead,§ – of Henry

*See Anti-Slavery Reporter, nos. 5 and 16.
†Ibid, No. 44.
‡Ibid, No. 47.
§Ibid, No. 64, p. 345; no. 71, p. 481.

Williams,‖ – and of the Rev. Mr. Bridges and Kitty
Hylton,* in Jamaica. These cases alone might suffice to
demonstrate the inevitable tendency of slavery as it exists
in our colonies, to brutalize the master to a truly frightful
degree – a degree which would often cast into the shade
even the atrocities related in the narrative of Mary Prince;
and which are sufficient to prove, independently of all
other evidence, that there is nothing in the revolting
character of the facts to affect their credibility; but that
on the contrary, similar deeds are at this very time of
frequent occurrence in almost every one of our slave
colonies. The system of coercive labour may vary in
different places; it may be more destructive to human life
in the cane culture of Mauritius and Jamaica, than in the
predial and domestic bondage of Bermuda or the
Bahamas, – but the spirit and character of slavery are
every where the same, and cannot fail to produce similar
effects. Wherever slavery prevails, there will inevitably be
found cruelty and oppression. Individuals who have
preserved humane, and amiable, and tolerant dispositions
towards their black dependents, may doubtless be found
among slave-holders; but even where a happy instance of
this sort occurs, such as Mary's first mistress, the kind-
hearted Mrs. Williams, the favoured condition of the slave
is still as precarious as it is rare: it is every moment at the
mercy of events; and must always be held by a tenure so
proverbially uncertain as that of human prosperity, or
human life. Such examples, like a feeble and flickering
streak of light in a gloomy picture, only serve by contrast
to exhibit the depth of the prevailing shades. Like other
exceptions, they only prove the general rule: the unquestionable tendency of the system is to vitiate the best
tempers, and to harden the most feeling hearts. 'Never be

‖Ibid, No. 65, p. 356; no. 69, p. 431.
*Anti-Slavery Reporter, Nos. 66, 69, and 76.

kind, nor speak kindly to a slave,' said an accomplished English lady in South Africa to my wife: 'I have now,' she added, 'been for some time a slave-owner, and have found, from vexatious experience in my own household, that nothing but harshness and hauteur will do with slaves.'

I might perhaps not inappropriately illustrate this point more fully by stating many cases which fell under my own personal observation, or became known to me through authentic sources, at the Cape of Good Hope – a colony where slavery assumes, as it is averred, a milder aspect than in any other dependency of the empire where it exists; and I could shew, from the judicial records of that colony, received by me within these few weeks, cases scarcely inferior in barbarity to the worst of those to which I have just specially referred; but to do so would lead me too far from the immediate purpose of this pamphlet, and extend it to an inconvenient length. I shall therefore content myself with quoting a single short passage from the excellent work of my friend Dr. Walsh, entitled 'Notices of Brazil,' – a work which, besides its other merits, has vividly illustrated the true spirit of Negro Slavery, as it displays itself not merely in that country, but wherever it has been permitted to open its Pandora's box of misery and crime.

Let the reader ponder on the following just remarks, and compare the facts stated by the Author in illustration of them, with the circumstances related at pages 56 and 57 of Mary's narratives:-

'If then we put out of the question the injury inflicted on others, and merely consider the deterioration of feeling and principle with which it operates on ourselves, ought it not to be a sufficient, and, indeed, unanswerable, argument, against the permission of Slavery?

'The exemplary manner in which the paternal duties are performed at home, may mark people as the most fond and affectionate parents; but let them once go abroad, and come within the contagion of slavery, and it seems to alter the very nature of a man; and the father has sold, and still sells, the mother and his children, with as little compunction as he would a sow and her litter of pigs; and he often disposes of them together.

'This deterioration of feeling is conspicuous in many ways among the Brazilians. They are naturally a people of a humane and good-natured disposition, and much indisposed to cruelty or severity of any kind. Indeed, the manner in which many of them treat their slaves is a proof of this, as it is really gentle and considerate; but the natural tendency to cruelty and oppression in the human heart, is continually evolved by the impunity and uncontrolled licence in which they are exercised. I never walked through the streets of Rio, that some house did not present to me the semblance of a bridewell, where the moans and the cries of the sufferers, and the sounds of whips and scourges within, announced to me that corporal punishment was being inflicted. Whenever I remarked this to a friend, I was always answered that the refractory nature of the slave rendered it necessary, and no house could properly be conducted unless it was practised. But this is certainly not the case; and the chastisement is constantly applied in the very wantonness of barbarity, and would not, and dared not, be inflicted on the humblest wretch in society, if he was not a slave, and so put out of the pale of pity.

'Immediately joining our house was one occupied by a mechanic, from which the most dismal cries and moans constantly proceeded. I entered the shop one day, and found it was occupied by a saddler, who had two negro boys working at his business. He was a tawny, cadaverous-looking man, with a dark aspect; and he had cut from his leather a scourge like a Russian knout, which he held in his hand, and was in the act of exercising on one of the naked children in an inner room: and this was the cause of the moans and cries we heard every day, and almost all day long.

'In the rear of our house was another, occupied by some women of bad character, who kept, as usual, several negro slaves. I was awoke early one morning by dismal cries, and looking out of the window, I saw in the back yard of the house, a black girl of about fourteen years old; before her stood her mistress, a white woman, with a large stick in her hand. She was undressed except her petticoat and chemise, which had fallen down and left her shoulders and bosom bare. Her hair was streaming behind, and every fierce and malevolent passion was depicted in her face. She too, like my hostess at Governo [another striking illustration of the *dehumanizing* effects of Slavery,] was the very representation of a fury. She was striking the poor girl, whom she had driven up into a corner, where she was on her knees appealing for mercy. She shewed her none, but continued to strike her on the head and thrust the stick into her face, till she was herself exhausted, and her poor victim covered with blood. This scene was renewed every morning, and the cries and moans of the poor suffering blacks, announced that they were enduring the penalty of slavery in being the objects on which the irritable and malevolent passions of the whites are allowed to vent themselves with impunity; nor could I help deeply deploring that state of society in which the vilest characters in the community are allowed an almost uncontrolled power of life and death, over their innocent, and far more estimable fellow-creatures.' – (Notices of Brazil, vol. ii. p. 354-356.)

In conclusion, I may observe that the history of Mary
Prince furnishes a corollary to Lord Stowell's decision in
the case of the slave Grace, and that it is most valuable on
this account. Whatever opinions may be held by some
readers on the grave question of immediately abolishing
Colonial Slavery, nothing assuredly can be more repug-
nant to the feelings of Englishmen than that the system
should be permitted to extend its baneful influence to this
country. Yet such is the case, when the slave landed in
England still only possesses that qualified degree of
freedom, that a change of domicile will determine it.
Though born a British subject, and resident within the
shores of England, he is cut off from his dearest natural
rights by the sad alternative of regaining them at the
expence of liberty, and the certainty of severe treatment.
It is true that he has the option of returning; but it is a
cruel mockery to call it a voluntary choice, when upon his
return depend his means of subsistence and his re-union
with all that makes life valuable. Here he has tasted 'the
sweets of freedom,' to quote the words of the unfortunate
Mary Prince; but if he desires to restore himself to his
family, or to escape from suffering and destitution, and
the other evils of a climate uncongenial to his constitution
and habits, he must abandon the enjoyment of his late-
acquired liberty, and again subject himself to the
arbitrary power of a vindictive master.

The case of Mary Prince is by no means a singular one;
many of the same kind are daily occurring; and even if
the case were singular, it would still loudly call for the
interference of the legislature. In instances of this kind no
injury can possibly be done to the owner by confirming to
the slave his resumption of his natural rights. It is the
master's spontaneous act to bring him to this country; he
knows when he brings him that he divests himself of his
property; and it is, in fact, a minor species of slave
trading, when he has thus enfranchised his slave, to *re-*

capture that slave by the necessities of his condition, or by working upon the better feelings of his heart. Abstracted from all legal technicalities, there is no real difference between thus compelling the return of the enfranchised negro, and trepanning a free native of England by delusive hopes into perpetual slavery. The most ingenious casuist could not point out any essential distinction between the two cases. Our boasted liberty is the dream of imagination, and no longer the characteristic of our country, if its bulwarks can thus be thrown down by colonial special pleading. It would well become the character of the present Government to introduce a Bill into the Legislature making perpetual that freedom which the slave has acquired by his passage here, and thus to declare, in the most ample sense of the words, (what indeed we had long fondly believed to be the fact, though it now appears that we have been mistaken,) THAT NO SLAVE CAN EXIST WITHIN THE SHORES OF GREAT BRITAIN.

APPENDIXES

APPENDIX 1

Mary Prince's Petition Presented to Parliament on June 24, 1829

I thank D.J. Johnson, Deputy Clerk of the Records, Record Office, House of Lords, for a photocopy of the following petition. It appears in *Common Journal LXXXIV*, p. 404, under date 19 June 1829. Mr Wood almost had his way in not having the petition presented for Parliament and prorogued five days later on 24th June.*

PETITION

A Petition of **Mary Prince** or **James**, commonly called **Molly Wood**, was presented, and read; setting forth, That the Petitioner was born a Slave in the colony of **Bermuda**, and is now about forty years of age; That the Petitioner was sold some years go for the sum of 300 dollars to Mr **John Wood**, by whom the Petitioner was carried to **Antigua**, where she has since, until lately resided as a domestic slave on his establishment; that in December 1826, the Petitioner who is connected with the **Moravian** Congregation, was married in a **Moravian** Chapel at **Spring Gardens**, in the parish of **Saint John's**, by the **Moravian** minister, Mr **Ellesen**, to a free Black of the name of **Daniel James**, who is a carpenter at **Saint John's**, in **Antigua**, and also a member of the same congregation; that the Petitioner and the said **Daniel James** have lived together ever since as man and wife; that about ten months ago the Petitioner arrived in **London**, with her master and mistress, in the capacity of nurse to their child; that the Petitioner's master has offered

---

*This petition was another successful element in Mary Prince's ultimate ability to turn the tables on the Woods. In the petition-exposé as in the narrative, she is a public spokeswoman for all slaves against all slavemasters, impugning their reputations in the very society in which they seek to vindicate themselves and slavery.

to send her back in his brig to the **West Indies** , to work in the yard; that the Petitioner expressed her desire to return to the **West Indies,** but not as a slave, and has entreated her master to sell her, her freedom on account of her services as a nurse to his child, but he has refused, and still does refuse; further stating the particulars of her case; and praying the House to take the same into their consideration, and to grant such relief as to them may, under the circumstances, appear right. **Ordered,** That the said Petition do lie upon the Table.

Postscript to the Second Edition

A postscript to the second edition (no copy of which I have yet found) is included in the prefatory apparatus to the third edition, is dated March 22, 1831, and reads as follows:

POSTSCRIPT – SECOND EDITION

Since the First Edition of this Tract was published, Mary Prince has been afflicted with a disease in the eyes, which, it is feared, may terminate in total blindness: such, at least, is the apprehension of some skilful medical gentlemen who have been consulted on the case. Should this unfortunately be the result, the condition of the poor negro woman, thus cruelly and hopelessly severed from her husband and her home, will be one peculiarly deserving of commiseration; and I mention the circumstance at present on purpose to induce the friends of humanity to promote the more zealously the sale of this publication, with a view to provide a little fund for her future benefit. Whatever be the subsequent lot that Providence may have in reserve for her, the seasonable sympathy thus manifested on her behalf, will neither be fruitlessly expended nor unthankfully received; while, in accordance with the benign Scripture mandate, it will serve to mitigate and relieve, as far as human kindness can, the afflictions of 'the stranger and the exile who is in our land within our gates'.

Appendix to the Third Edition

The following was appended after the end of the text of the third edition.

APPENDIX

[As inquiries has been made from various quarters respecting the existence of marks of severe punishment on Mary Prince's body, it seems proper to append to this Edition, the following letter on that subject, written by Mrs Pringle to Mrs Townsend, one of the benevolent Secretaries of the 'Birmingham Ladies' Society for Relief of Negro Slaves'.]

'London, 7 Solly Terrace, Claremont Square,
March 28, 1831.

'Dear Madam,

'My husband having read to me the passage in your last letter to him, expressing a desire to be furnished with some description of the marks of former ill-usage on Mary Prince's person, – I beg in reply to state, that the whole of the back part of her body is distinctly scarred, and, as it were, *chequered*, with the vestiges of severe floggings. Besides this, there are many large scars on other parts of her person, exhibiting an appearance as if the flesh had been deeply cut, or lacerated with *gashes*, by some instrument wielded by most unmerciful hands. Mary affirms, that all these scars were occasioned by the various cruel punishments she has mentioned or referred to in her narrative; and of the entire truth of this statement I have no hesitation in declaring myself perfectly satisfied, not only from my dependence on her uniform veracity, but also from my previous observation of similar cases at the Cape of Good Hope.

'In order to put you in possession of such full and authentic evidence, respecting the marks on Mary Prince's person, as may serve your benevolent purpose in making the inquiry, I beg to add to my own testimony that of Miss Strickland (the lady who wrote down in this house the narratives of Mary Prince and Ashton Warner), together with the testimonies of my sister Susan and my friend Miss Martha Browne – all of whom were present and assisted me this day in a second inspection of Mary's body.

'I remain, Dear Madam,
   'Yours very truly,
     'M. PRINGLE.'

'The above statement is certified and corroborated by
     'SUSANNA STRICKLAND,
     'SUSAN BROWN
     'MARTHA A. BROWNE.'

To
  Mrs Townsend,
    West-Bromwich,
      Birmingham.

'Narrative of Louis Asa-Asa, a Captured African'

The following narrative is included at the end of Mary Prince's *History* in every edition, with prefatory comment presumably by Thomas Pringle. In its description of the kidnapping in Africa and the Middle Passage, it conforms in miniature to an orthodox pattern of African male slave narratives.

NARRATIVE OF LOUIS ASA-ASA
A captured African

The following interesting narrative is a convenient supplement to the history of Mary Prince. It is given, like hers, as nearly as possible in the narrator's words, with only so much correction as was necessary to connect the story, and render it grammatical. The concluding passage in inverted commas, is entirely his own. While Mary's narrative shews the disgusting character of colonial slavery, this little tale explains with equal force the horrors in which it originates.

It is necessary to explain that Louis came to this country about five years ago, in a French vessel called the Pearl. She had lost her reckoning, and was driven by stress of weather into the port of St Ives, in Cornwall. Louis and his four companions were brought to London upon a writ of Habeas Corpus at the instance of Mr George Stephen; and after some trifling opposition on the part of the master of the vessel, were discharged by Lord Wynford. Two of his unfortunate fellow-sufferers died of the measles at Hampstead; the other two returned to Sierra Leone; but, poor Louis, when offered the choice of going back to Africa, replied, 'Me no father, no mother now; me stay with you.' And here he has ever since remained; conducting himself in a way to gain the good will and respect of all who know him. He is remarkably intelligent, understands our language perfectly, and can read and write well. The last sentences of the following narrative will seem almost too peculiar to be his own; but it is not the first time that in conversation with Mr George Stephen, he has made similar remarks. On one occasion in particular, he was heard saying to himself in the kitchen, while sitting by the fire apparently in deep thought, 'Me think, – me think – ' A fellow–servant inquired what he meant; and he added, 'Me think what a good thing I came to England! Here, I know what God is, and read my Bible; in my country they have no God, no Bible.'

How severe and just a reproof to the guilty wretches who visit his country only with fire and sword! How deserved a censure upon the not less guilty men, who dare to vindicate the state of slavery, on the lying pretext, that its victims are of an inferior nature! And scarcely less deserving of reprobation are those who have it in their power to prevent these crimes, but who remain inactive from indifference, or are dissuaded from throwing the shield of British power over the victim of oppression, by the sophistry, and the clamour, and the avarice of the oppressor. It is the reproach and the sin of England. May God avert from our country the ruin which this national guilt deserves!

We lament to add, that the Pearl which brought these negroes to our shore, was restored to its owners at the instance of the French Government, instead of being condemned as a prize to Lieutenant Rye, who, on his own responsibility, detained her, with all her manacles and chains and other detestable proofs of her piratical occupation on board. We trust it is not yet too late to demand investigation into the reasons for restoring her.

THE NEGRO BOY'S NARRATIVE

My father's name was Clashoquin; mine is Asa-Asa. He lived in a country called Bycla, near Egie, a large town. Egie is as large as Brighton; it was some way from the sea. I had five brothers and sisters. We all lived together with my father and mother; he kept a horse, and was respectable, but not one of the great men. My uncle was one of the great men at Egie; he could make men come and work for him; his name was Otou. He had a great deal of land and cattle. My father sometimes worked on his own land, and used to make charcoal. I was too little to work; my eldest brother used to work on the land; and we were all very happy.

A great many people, whom we called Adinyes, set fire to Egie in the morning before daybreak; there were some thousands of them. They killed a great many, and burnt all their houses. They staid two days, and then carried away all the people whom they did not kill.

They came again every now and then for a month, as long as they could find people to carry away. They used to tie them by the feet, except when they were taking them off, and then they let them loose; but if they offered to run away, they would shoot them. I lost a great many friends and relatives at Egie; about a dozen. They sold all they carried away, to be slaves. I know this because I afterwards saw them as slaves on the other side of the sea. They took away brothers, and sisters, and husbands, and wives; they did not care about this. They were sold for cloth or gunpowder, sometimes for salt or guns; sometimes they got four or five guns for a man: they were English guns, made like a master's that I clean for his shooting. The Adinyes burnt a great many places besides Egie. They burnt all the country wherever they found villages; they used to shoot men, women, and children, if they ran away.

They came to us about eleven o'clock one day, and directly they came they set our house on fire. All of us had run away. We kept together, and went into the woods, and stopped there two days. The Adinyes then went away, and we returned home and found every thing burnt. We tried to build a little shed, and were beginning to get comfortable again. We found several of our neighbours lying about wounded; they had been shot. I saw the bodies of four or five little children whom they had killed with blows on the head. They had carried away their fathers and mothers, but the children were too small for slaves, so they killed them. They had killed several others, but these were all that I saw. I saw them lying in the street like dead dogs.

In about a week after we got back, the Adinyes returned, and burnt all the sheds and houses they had left standing. We all ran away again; we went to the woods as we had done before. – They followed us the next day. We went farther into the woods, and staid there about four days and nights: we were half starved; we only got a few potatoes. My uncle Otou was with us. At the end of this time, the Adinyes found us. We ran away. They called my uncle to go to them; but he refused, and they shot him immediately: they killed him. The rest of us ran on, and they did not get at us till the next day. I ran up into a tree; they followed me and brought me down. They tied my feet. I do not know if they found my father and mother, and brothers and sisters: they had run faster than me, and were half a mile farther when I got up into the tree: I have never seen them since. – There was a man who ran up into the tree with me: I believe they shot him, for I never saw him again.

They carried away about twenty besides me. They carried us to the sea. They did not beat us: they only killed one man, who was very ill and too weak to carry his load; they made all of us carry chickens and meat for our food; but this poor man could not carry his load, and they ran him through the body with a sword. – He was a neighbour of ours. When we got to the sea they sold all of us, but not to the same person. They sold us for money; and I was sold six times over, sometimes for money, sometimes for cloth, and sometimes for a gun. I was about thirteen years old. It was about half a year from the time I was taken, before I saw the white people.

We were taken in a boat from place to place, and sold at every place we stopped at. In about six months we got to a ship, in which we first saw white people: they were French. They bought us. We found here a great many other slaves; there were about eighty, including women and children. The Frenchmen sent away all but five of us into another very large ship. We five staid on board till we got to England, which was about five or six months. The slaves we saw on board the ship were chained together by the legs below deck, so close they could not move. They were flogged very cruelly: I saw one of them flogged till he died; we could not tell what for. They gave them enough to eat. The place they were confined in below deck was so hot and nasty I could not bear to be in it. A great many of the slaves were ill, but they were not attended to. They used to flog me very bad on board the ship: the captain cut my head very bad one time.

'I am very happy to be in England, as far as I am very well; – but I have no friend belonging to me, but God, who will take care of me as he has done already. I am very glad I have come to England, to know who God is. I should like much to see my friends again, but I do not now wish to go back to them; for if I go back to my own country, I might be taken as a slave again. I would rather stay here, where I am free, than go back to my country to be sold. I shall stay in England as long as (please God) I shall live. I wish the King of England could know all I have told you. I wish it that he may see how cruelly we are used. We had no king in our country, or he would have stopt it. I think the King of England might stop it, and this is why I wish him to know it all. I have heard say he is good; and if he is, he will stop it if he can. I am well off myself, for I am well taken care of, and have good bed and good clothes; but I wish my own people to be as comfortable.

APPENDIX 5

Court Case Involving Mary Prince
Pringle v. Cadell

February 21, 1833

This was an action brought by Mr. Pringle, the secretary to the Anti-Slavery Society, against the defendant, for a libel published in *Blackwood's Magazine.*

Mr. Richards having opened the pleadings, Mr. Sergeant Welde, who was further assisted by Mr. Serjeant Jones, stated the plaintiff's case to the jury. The plaintiff, he said was a respectable gentleman in this city. The defendant, Mr. Cadell, was the London publisher of *Blackwood's Magazine,* a work having considerable circulation, and conducted with some talent. Mr. Pringle filled the situation of secretary to an association of persons who subscribed together for the purpose of furnishing the public with information on the subject of negro slavery in the West Indies. Upon this subject considerable difference of opinion existed in this country. There was one class of persons who thought that the existence of slavery in our colonial possessions was not inconsistent with those principles of liberty which were so highly valued by the British nation: there was another class of persons who thought that the slaves ought to be relieved from their unhappy condition. It was not for him to pronounce any judgement as to which of those opinions was the right one, because that was a question the consideration of which formed no part of the business of today. Mr. Pringle had published a pamphlet containing the statement of a negro woman, named Mary Prince, as to the treatment she had received from her owners in the West Indies, which pamphlet had been so published by him, not as connected with the association, but on his own individual judgment and responsibility. Now, it was very well known that there was a numerous and powerful party, consisting of the white population in the West Indies, and those

136

whose interests were connected with them, who left no measure untried, either by intimidation, or oppression, or calumny, to prevent any correct information as to the state and condition of the slaves from being given to the public. The defence to-day [*sic*], he had no doubt, although conducted in Mr. Cadell's name, was substantially the defence of that party. It was their interests, and not his own, that Mr. Cadell was defending to-day. When the plaintiff first brought this action, and thereby challenged the defendant to substantiate, if he could, the imputations cast upon him, the defendant accepted the challenge, and by his pleas justified the truth of the libel. Perhaps he did that in order to terrify the plaintiff by the expense to which he should be put in meeting those pleas by evidence. Now, however, when the cause came down for trial, he abandoned all those pleas, and rested on the general issue, merely denying the publication. The jury were aware that from the situation of the slaves in the West Indies, and the distance of those colonies from here, it was extremely difficult to obtain correct information on that subject. The slave Mary Prince having come to this country, Mr. Pringle met her, or perhaps sought her out, and having heard from her mouth a statement of the treatment she had received, he published it. Now, it was perfectly competent for the defendant, or anybody else, to say of the facts contained in that statement that they were false; but the defendant, not content with doing that, had thought proper to impute intentional falsehood and gross misconduct to the plaintiff. A magazine was not like a newspaper, which might be read to-day and forgotten too-morrow [*sic*]; it was a publication of a more permanent character, and therefore the more likely to effect a lasting injury on the character which it attacked. The libel in question was contained in an article purporting to be a letter from a Mr. McQueen to Lord Grey, and reflected in the grossest manner, not only upon the plaintiff; but even attacked the ladies of his family. Here the learned serjeant read some passages from the article in question. It professed to be a reply to the pamphlet published by the plaintiff, whom it described as "the sell-known Mr. Pringle," and alleged that he had taken that wretched tool, Mary Prince, from the wash-tub to the closet, for the purpose of collecting the filthy statement of her lies and immorality, and impressing it on the minds of his own family. The learned serjeant having commented on this publication, said, that Mary Prince was in court, and he should put her into the box, to allow his learned friends on the other side an opportunity of cross-examining her if they pleased. After some further observations, he concluded by calling on the jury to give a verdict for such damages as the plaintiff was in justice entitled to as compensation for the unwarrantable accusation which had been brought against him.

Mr. George Stephen, the attorney for the plaintiff, produced a copy of *Blackwood's Magazine,* dated November, 1831, which he had purchased from the defendant. This was solely the action of the plaintiff personally.

Cross-examined,—Witness had acted occasionally for the anti-Slavery Society, but always gratuitously.

The libel was then put in and read. It extended to a great length, [and] professed, amongst other things, to expose what it termed the black system of falsehood against the colonists. The greater part of it consisted of animadversions on Mary Prince's statement.

Mary Prince was then called in and sworn. She is a negress of very ordinary features, and appeared to be about 35 years of age. She stated that she gave an account of her life to Mr. Pringle. No other question was put to her by the plaintiff's counsel, and the other side declined to cross-examine her.

Mr. Serjeant Coleridge (who was assisted by Mr. Follett) addressed the jury at considerable length on behalf of the defendant. Notwithstanding the disdain of Mr. Serjeant Wilde, he thought there was something more in the case than the mere object which had been avowed. The question which had been alluded to by his learned friend was a great and important one, which, however, would be agitated where it ought to be agitated, in the great council of the nation, and also by the public press, but they had nothing to do with it in court of justice. Everybody was aware that on the one hand there existed a party in this country who were endeavouring to effect the emancipation of the slaves at once, whilst, on the other hand, there was a large body who were anxious to preserve vested interests in the colonies. There was an intermediate party, whose desire it was that the freedom of the slaves might be worked out by safe and gradual, though by rapid measures. Whichever of these parties might be right, he agreed with his learned brother that the jury had nothing to do with the question. It had been said that the jury, dismission all feelings on the general question from their minds, ought to try the case on the evidence produced before them; but they would not be doing so if they took Mr. Cadell as the organ of the powerful party to whom Mr. Serjeant Wilde had alluded. The plaintiff was a respectable man, the London publisher of an Edinburgh magazine, as he might be of the *Edinburgh Review,* or any other periodical work, of the contents of which he knew no more before it was published than any one of the jury. At the same time, he admitted that as such publisher he was legally responsible for any libels it might contain; but let him not, therefore, be taken to be connected with any party. The learned serjeant then proceeded comment on the libel, contending that it was a fair discussion of a subject on which the plaintiff had himself published a statement reflecting on the character of respectable persons, and one of these a lady, although he was so very tender of any allusion to his own family. The author took this up as a specimen to show Lord Grey the manner in which the colonists were attacked; and his commentary upon it strictly fell within the fair scope of argument, with the exception, perhaps, of one or two expressions which would have been better omitted, and for which, as they could not be justified, the plaintiff was entitled to a verdict; but he contended that under all the circumstances nominal damages would satisfy the justice of the case.

The learned Judge having summed up the case,

The Jury returned a verdict for the plaintiff—Damages £3.

Court Case Involving Mary Prince
Wood v. Pringle

March 1, 1833

This was an action for libel. The defendant pleaded, besides the general issue, a justification to the greater part of the declaration.

Sir J. Scarlett said this was an action to recover compensation in damages for certain libels contained in a pamphlet published by the defendant affecting the character of the plaintiff. The defendant (Mr. Pringle) was secretary to the Anti-Slavery Society, who, as the jury were aware, were associated for the purpose of exciting public feeling on the subject of slavery in the West Indies. The plaintiff (Mr. John Adams Wood) was a proprietor of slaves, and one who wished for their emancipation as much as the Anti-Slavery Society, or any other persons, could do; at the same time he entertained an opinion, in common with many others, that to effect an emancipation suddenly would be productive of nothing but ruin both—masters and slaves. The libels of which the plaintiff complained arose out of the circumstances which he would shortly detail to the jury. Mr. and Mrs. Wood, who resided at Antigua, became possessed of a female slave of the name of Mary Prince, who lived with them at Antigua until they had occasion to come to England, when she was, at her own request, brought over with them. On coming to England Mr. and Mrs. Wood took up their residence in Leigh-street, near Brunswick-square, and Mary Prince remained with them some time, until she complained that the work which was allotted to her was much more laborious than any she had ever been accustomed to in Antigua, and she was at length discharged, after an offer made to her by Mr. and Mrs. Wood that she might return to Antigua if she wished. She then entered into the service of Mr. Pringle (the defendant), and soon afterwards the pamphlet in question appeared. The learned counsel proceeded to read the passages in the pamphlet in question, which ascribed to the plaintiff and his wife a series of misconduct and cruelty towards Mary Prince, and he pointed out those parts of the libel which he said the defendant had not attempted to justify. He should be able to prove, by the evidence of the plaintiff's daughters, and also by a medical man, that Mary Prince had always been treated with kindness, and had had medical attendance when ill at Antigua. If the defendant should fail to make out his justification, by proving the truth of the statement, the plaintiff would be entitled to a verdict, and the jury would then have to consider only one question—vix., what amount of damages would be fit and proper for them to award against the defendant for such a publication.

The pamphlet was put in and read: it purported to be a "narrative of the history of Mary Prince, a negro slave, taken from her own statements;" and to the "narrative" were added comments by the defendant. The "narrative" consisted of a statement of the alleged sufferings of Mary Prince from her birth in the Bermudas, during her residence in Antigua and Turk's Island, until her introduction to the defendant and the Anti-Slavery society. It was stated that a paper had been given to her by the plaintiff, previously to her leaving him in London, offering her either a return to Antigua or to remain in his service in England if she was disposed to work, but stating that, as she had shown a disinclination to work, he could not continue to pay her wages as a servant, nor allow her to remain in his house. This paper was commented on in the pamphlet as being an artifice, to prevent the girl from being engaged by any other person in England, and thereby compel her to return to Antigua, at which place she would become a slave. It was also stated in the pamphlet that after the plaintiff's return to England an offer had been made to the plaintiff by the Anti-Slavery society, through the governor, to procure her manumission, which it was said was refused by the plaintiff, for reasons stated in a letter to the secretary of the governor, which letter was published in the pamphlet. One of the reasons was the alleged depravity of Mary Prince, to which it was said Mr. Dyer, a magistrate, of Antigua, was able to speak; but the passage relating an instance of the girl's depravity was omitted in the pamphlet, and the plaintiff's statement was treated as untrue. The pamphlet also stated that the girl (who had been married to a free black in Antigua) had been incited by the plaintiff to be unfaithful to her husband, in order that that circumstance might be made use of against her as an instance of depravity; and the pamphlet also alleged that a statement which the plaintiff had made, to the effect that the free black had been himself unfaithful, and had taken another wife, was false, and had been invented for the purpose of inducing Mary Prince to desert her husband. The pamphlet stated also, that the opinion of the defendant and his family (formed after a long service on the part of Mary Prince) was, that she was a faithful and useful servant, and that, in fact, her conduct was directly the reverse of that which had been ascribed to her by the plaintiff.

[We have been furnished with a copy of the pamphlet, but the detail which it contains relating to the plaintiff and his wife is much too long for publication by us; and there is perhaps the less necessity for publishing it as the greater part of the girl's statement respecting her master and mistress's treatment of her is given in her evidence for the defence.]

Mrs. Sarah Pell stated, that she resided in Antigua about 12 years ago. She knew Mr. and Mrs. Wood intimately, and frequently stayed with them as a guest. The general conduct of Mr. Wood towards his slaves was everything that was kind, and Mrs. Wood appeared to be of a very mild temper. Witness' never knew of any instance of Mr. Wood flogging his slaves. He did not appear to be what the libel had characterized him—"a vindictive man;" on the contrary, he always appeared very mild in his treatment of the slaves. Witness knew Mr. and Mrs. Wood in the year 1828, in Leigh-street, and saw Mary Prince there. Witness called at the house accidentally, and found her about to leave, and asked her to go out with her. Witness then begged her to conduct herself well for a few days at her master's, and then come to her (witness) at Brixton, while Mr. and Mrs. Wood were at Cheltenhem, but she refused. The witness was next examined as to the truth of the statements contained in the pamphlet, and contradicted them. She received a copy of the pamphlet from the defendant, accompanied by a letter, stating that as she was understood to object to certain statements in it, he could insert her remarks in a note. Witness replied, by letter, that she would rather not have her observations appended; but that she regretted that such statements should have been made against Mr. and Mrs. Wood, whose characters were so very different from that imputed to them. The defendant, in his reply, requested an appointment to examine Mary Prince as to the truth of her statements.

The letter, together with the witness's reply, declining the inquiry, was read.

Cross-examined.—Witness was at Mr. and Mrs. Wood's on a visit, only a week while they were at home, and she was there a short time after they left home. Was never in any other West Indies Island, and never saw any slaves punished. Had seen a field of slaves at work with an overseer, but never saw a whip in his hands, to her recollection. Witness was willing to have taken Mary Prince into her service. Had heard of her being very provoking to her mistress, and giving her a great deal of trouble. Mr. and Mrs. Wood left England in the beginning of 1829.

Robert Briggs, Esq., stated that he was magistrate in Antigua, where he had resided for about 30 years. He resided 11 miles from St. John's, where Mr. Wood lived. The number of white inhabitants was about

1,500, and they were well known to each other. Witness had known Mr. Wood since the year 1806. He had visited Mr. and Mrs. Wood, and resided with them several times. They were always very mild and gentle to their servants, who were well dressed, and did anything for Mr. and Mrs. Wood's guests very cheerfully. Mary Prince was well dressed, and always appeared cheerful and satisfied. By the laws of Antigua a master who is too severe with his slaves is liable to punishment.

Cross-examined.—Witness was indicted in 1831 for a cruelty to his slaves and acquitted. He resigned his office of magistrate voluntarily in 1832. He had been complained of by a Mr. Leving, together with all the authorities of the island, for misconduct as a magistrate, and cruelty to slaves. He had slaves punished, and had perhaps striped them himself with a whip, if put out of temper. He remembered a body of 100 or 200 slaves coming to the governor to complain of ill-treatment by drivers whom witness had appointed. That was in Antigua, 1831, when witness was a magistrate. Witness was a slave-master, not a slave-owner. He went on the estate in question in 1802, and no complaint was made of him until the time he had mentioned.

Re-examined.—He applied at the Colonial-office to know whether any charge had been preferred against him by Mr. Loving, and received a letter from Lord Howick, on the 20th of February, stating that he was worry he had taken so much trouble, as there was no charge against him.

Dr. John M'Goul stated, that he resided at Antigua, and was a member of the Legislative Assembly. He had attended Mr. Wood and his family for nearly 15 years. He knew Mary Prince, who had been put under his care as a medical man. He never saw greater attention and kindness paid to any one than were paid to her by Mr. and Mrs. Wood. She appeared to be favourite with her mistress. She had every comfort as regarded bed and bedding, and there was a mosquito net. She was always very well dressed. She had a complaint called St. Anthony's fire. Witness attended her for a long time, and she had every care necessary for her recovery. Witness had frequently seen Mrs. Wood attending on her, and giving her food with her own hands. The witness contradicted several statements in the pamphlet of the ill-treatment of Mary Prince.

Cross-examined.—Witness was a proprietor of slaves, and had seen slaves punished. Never ordered more than a dozen and a half or two dozen lashes. Was dismissed from his office of magistrate about two months after his arrival in England on an *ex parte* statement, which he was able to disprove by documents. Witness directed the use of the whip as little as possible, and generally ordered confinement.

[Witness was shown a plan of the plaintiff's house, and also in its place of the separate abode of Mary Prince, which he identified.]

Mrs. Mary Caroline Bennet stated that she was a daughter of Mr. and Mrs. Wood. She left Antigua in 1824, and was married last April. She remembered Mary Prince living in her father's family, and she taught her to read the Bible. The girl was very kindly used indeed; and witness never knew an instance of her father or mother ill-treating her. Her bedroom was furnished very well, and her house was not "a dirty out-house" as stated in the pamphlet: it was quite the contrary. Mrs. Wood always treated Mary Prince with the utmost kindness, and attended to her herself. She had money allowed her, and was always very well dressed. The witness contradicted certain statements in the pamphlet as to the cruel treatment of Mary Prince. Witness was with her father and mother in Leigh-street. They had two white servants and two black ones. There was no diminution of kindness towards Mary Prince, but she appeared very discontented. She did not like roast beef and veal, because she thought it was horse-flesh; that was the first ground for discontent. She appeared to perform her work very unwillingly. She once had a piece of linen given to her which she refused to wash. A charwoman was always hired to assist in the washing. (This portion of the evidence was for the purpose of contradicting specific statements in the pamphlet.) Mary Prince went away voluntarily, and not in conse-quence of any harsh treatment on the part of Mr. and Mrs. Wood.

Cross-Examined.—Witness did not know that her father had been indemnitied in bringing this action. Never heard of any charge of immo-rality against Mary Prince. Witness had heard her father say that it was Dr. Lushington's wish that Mary Prince should be manumitted.

Re-examined.—Witness had heard her father say that it was his inten-tion of Mary Prince had behaved well, to have given her her freedom on her return to Antigua.

Captain Henry Drysdale stated that he knew Mr. and Mrs. Wood well, and remembered their coming over to England in his vessel in June, 1828, Mary Prince being with them. Mary Prince fared during the voy-age as well as her mistress, and slept in the same cabin. Her treatment was in every respect humane, and witness never saw Mr. or Mrs. Wood harsh or severe with her. Mr. Wood was a most kind master, and a man of mild disposition. The witness contradicted several of the statements in the pamphlet as to the plaintiff's general disposition.

Cross-examined.—Mary Prince was very lazy, and witness had more trouble with her than any other person in the vessel. The plaintiff fre-quently complained of her conduct.

—Parry stated that he was Archdeacon of Antigua and the surround-ing islands. He arrived in Antigua in the year 1825. The characters of all persons of any consideration there were pretty well known. Witness always understood the plaintiff to be a man of unsullied reputation. He had known the plaintiff personally since the year 1829. He (the plaintiff) had been always forward in benevolent undertakings. Witness's opinion was different from the statement in the pamphlet as to the plaintiff's general temper and disposition.

On his cross-examination he stated that he never had any direct opportunity of judging of the plaintiff's treatment of his slaves.

This was the plaintiff's case.

The SOLICITOR-GENERAL addressed the jury for the defendant. He submitted that the evidence of most of the plaintiff's witnesses was not conclusive, and did not contradict the statements in the pamphlet. He said he should be able to substantiate those statements by the evidence of Mary Prince herself, and show that the treatment of her by Mr. and Mrs. Wood was such as to induce her to resolve never to return to Antigua, where she would have again become a slave. The learned counsel contended that nothing like malice could be imputed to the defendant in the publication of the pamphlet. It was put forth solely for the purpose of opening the eyes of the public to the sufferings of the slaves by the personal narrative of one of the sufferers. Those parts of the alleged libel which were not justified would be found in the unimportant.

Mary Prince was the first witness called for the defence. She stated that she was now living in the Old Bailey, and was supported by the defendant. She had been a slave of the plaintiff, who purchased her for 300 dollars. When the plaintiff first purchased her she had to perform the general duties of a servant in the house, as was afterwards employed in washing. She afterwards became ill with St. Anthony's fire and with the rheumatism. Her leg was much swollen and she could not walk without help. She slept at that time in one of the outhouses, where there were swarms of bugs. A Mrs. Green, who lived in the next yard, heard her cries in the outhouse; and she sent to her an old slave who used to bring her soup when she was ill. The doctor who attended her ordered her hot water. Brista, the cook, brought her dinner to the door of the outhouse, and then left her. The outhouse was very wet when it rained. The bed was stuffed with grass. The outhouse contained besides the bed a bench, which witness had brought from Bermuda, and a little old table. Witness seldom went out, and when she did go she walked with a stick a few yards from the outhouse. Letty occupied the adjoining room, and witness moved in there to the bath. Letty's room was better than her's. Dr. M'Goul saw her in that room. Mrs. Wood never visited witness in either room. Witness had a pig given to her for some money which was owing to her by a woman. She complained of this mode of payment to Mrs. Wood. Mr. Wood was sent for, and he hit witness two knocks, and told the woman to take the witness before the magistrate. On going before the magistrate the woman stated that Mr. Wood would not let her rest until she had made a complaint. Mr. Wood's nephew, Mr. Judkins, attended for Mr. Wood before the magistrate, who dismissed the complaint, and witness was afterwards flogged with a cat-o-nine-tails. She bled very much. The next morning she saw Mr. Wood, and begged him to sell her. She was afterwards taken before another magistrate, who decided in her favour. Mr. Wood and his family afterwards removed to a place called the Point. Witness had all the washing to do there. Mrs. Wood frequently called her a spawn, and a good-for-nothing devil. On one occasion Mrs. Wood followed her foot after foot, and scolded and rated. Mr. Wood was sent for, and he gave her a note to go and look for a person to buy her. The following day Mr. Wood beat her with a horsewhip. Martha Wilcox complained to Mrs. Wood, and Mrs. Wood said she would send for Mr. Wood, to give her 50 lashes; that she had been used to the whip, and should have it then. Mr. Wood then beat her all over her body. She was "joined by the Moravians" to Daniel James, who lived a short distance from Mr. Wood's house. Mr. Wood did not know of her marriage for three or four months. Mr. Burchell, a cooper, told him of it. Mr. Wood licked her for it. He gave her about 50 lashes, swore at her, and said he would not have a nigger man's clothes washed in the same tub with his. Mr. Burchell applied to purchase her, but Mr. Wood would not sell her. She and her husband were always very loving, but her mistress was fretful about it, and said she did not do work enough. Witness came over to England with Mrs. Wood, and had to take care of the child for her. On the passage Mrs. Wood told her she did not mean to treat her any better when she got to England. Witness was very ill on the passage with the rheumatism. She had all the washing to do in Leigh-street. After some time an old woman was hired, but witness continued to wash. She on one occasion said she wished they had sold her in Antigua, and not brought her to England. The plaintiff was in a great passion and turned her out of doors. Mrs. Wood never spoke to her kindly afterwards. She was always scolding her, calling her a devil, a black devil, and a spawn, and said she wanted to be a lady. Once, when she was so ill that she could not wash some clothes which had been given to her, the plaintiff told her that if she did not go away he would send her in the brig the next day to Antigua. She asked him to let her have her freedom, which he refused, saying she was free in England here, and as she liked to go out she might see what freedom would do for her in England. He told her that if she liked to return to Antigua she might, and take the consequences. She stayed in the house some time after the cook, a Mulatto woman, had gone away. When witness left the plaintiff's house the plaintiff gave her a paper which she gave to Mr. Stephen, the defendant's attorney. The cook read to her the paper, of which the plaintiff took a copy. She (witness) once lived with a Captain Abbot. The witness was here questioned as to a statement made by the plaintiff in a letter from him to the governor's secretary, published in the pamphlet, charging her with gross immorality, and she denied the truth of the statement. The history of her life was written down by Miss Strickland at her (witness's) request; and she told that lady the truth.

Cross-examined.—The defendant was paying her £10, or £12 a-week. He did this when she was out of place, and had done it since June last. The plaintiff gave witness the note soon after they came to England, and she continued in the plaintiff's service two months afterwards. She did not take the note to Mr. Stephen for some time. When she left the Bermudas for the West Indies she was about 20 years of age. She went with the plaintiff, who brought her at her own request, after about a year. Some years afterwards, when the plaintiff was about to sell her, she went on her knees and entreated Mrs. Wood to persuade him not to sell her. She did not mention the fact to Miss Strickland. The plaintiff's eldest daughter did not teach her to read the Bible; she was too wild. The youngest daughter taught her to read. She was christened by the Rev. Mr. Curtin, who told her to learn the Lord's Prayer. She got some of her neighbours to teach her it, and paid them. She knows Christmas time. The natives then have a "stir up;" they dress in white, and dance; but if the ministers know of their dancing they prevent it. The plaintiff gave her a note to the Rev. Mr. Curtin before she was christened, after she had begged for it and had been refused once. She was married about three years before she came to England. Her husband was a carpenter, a cooper, and a violin-player. The plaintiff gave him leave to live with her. She had lived seven years before with Captain Abbot. She did not live in the house with him, but slept with him sometimes in another hut which she had, in addition to her room in the plaintiff's yard. One night she found another woman in bed with the Captain in her house. This woman had pretended to be a friend of witness. (Laughter). Witness licked her, and she was obliged to get out of bed. (A laugh). The captain laughed, and the woman said she done it to plague witness. Witness took her next day to the Moravian black leader, when she denied it, and witness then licked her again. (A laugh). The woman then complained before a magistrate, Mr. Justice Dyett; and when the story was told, they all laughed, and the woman was informed that she must never come there again with such tales, or she would be put into the stocks. Witness was also before the justice about beating a female slave, respecting a pig. Witness did not beat the woman, but she was punished as though she did by the desire of Mr. and Mrs. Wood. She used to make a little money by selling small articles—such as coffee, yams, pigs, and c.; and she used to take in washing. She came to England at her own request. She knew a freeman of the name of Oyskman, who made a fool of her by telling her he would make her free. She lived with him for some time, but afterwards discharged him. That was when she first went to Antigua, and Oyskman was the first man who came to court her. She parted from Captain Abbot on his killing a man on board one of the plaintiff's vessels. She had been a member of the Moravian Society, and discharged herself in consequence of her connection with Captain Abbot.

She was kept out of the class for seven weeks. She told all this to Miss Strickland when that lady took down her narrative. These statements were not in the narrative published by the defendant. The slaves received presents at Christmas, and Mrs. Wood gave witness clothes.

Re-examined.—She received no wages when in Leigh-street.

Mr. Stephen, the defendant's attorney, produced a copy of the paper given by the plaintiff to Mary Prince; and stated that the action was not brought until 18 months after the first publication.

The plaintiff's letter to the Secretary of the Governor of Antigua was put in and read. It stated that Mary Prince's moral character was very bad, as the police records would show, and charged her with an act of gross indecency as a proof of her immoral conduct.

Mr. Phillips, a clerk in the Agency Anti-Slavery society's office, who produced the plaintiff's letter, stated, on his cross-examination, that he was the author of a letter containing comments on the narrative published in the pamphlet. He wrote it at the request of the defendant, to whom it was addressed. Witness had been in Antigua, and was imprisoned by the Speaker of the House of Assembly there for contempt; but the order was reversed by the Lord Goderich and Sir G. Murray. Witness had been fined by the magistrates there for striking a slave who had acted indecently. They could not do less than fine a person in witness's situation under the Amelioration Act.

Emma Hill stated that she was a laundress, and had been employed at the plaintiff's house on Leigh-street. The witness corroborated Mary Prince's statement as to the duty she had to perform there, and stated that the plaintiff of one occasion called her a d-- d lazy b--h.

Mr. H. W. Ravenscroft, an attorney, stated that in 1829 he made an application to the plaintiff to manumit Mary Prince, which he refused. Money was offered, but the plaintiff refused on any terms; and said he would not move a finger for her.

Susan Brown, a sister-in-law of Mary Prince, stated that she had examined her person, and found many marks of wounds upon her. She was as active as her state would allow; but she was so ill as to be hardly able to do any work.

Mr. Manning stated that he had had a correspondence with the plaintiff respecting Mary Prince. The plaintiff was disposed, on certain conditions, to manumit her, but did not wish to be driven to it by the interference of others.

With this evidence the defendant's case closed.

Sir JAMES SCARLETT then addressed the jury in reply. He contended that the testimony of Mary Prince was exaggerated, and did not go to destroy the positive testimony of the plaintiff's witnesses.

Verdict for the plaintiff on the whole issues—Damages £25.

Historical Slave Resistance in Bermuda

1656 November	Plot led by Black Tom and Cabilecto.
1673 December	Plot led by Robin and others.
1720–1731	"Poisoning Plots," including the one that Sarah Bassett allegedly led.
1761 October	Mingo and others initiate and lead a plot throughout Bermuda.

The Tread-Wheel

The erection of this machine being completed it was put in operation on Saturday week. When we visited it on Thursday last, LYDIA, (found guilty, in the Court of Quarter Sessions, of stealing a Doubloon, sentenced to one months imprisonment, and to be worked on the Tread-Wheel six times) was put on it, and continued for the space of ten minutes. . . . She evidently suffered considerably from the exertion, and when taken off, could not, without assistance, retain an upright position: when on the wheel she made several false steps, and stopped, but was soon made to continue her exercise. She was clad in a dress made for the purpose—a short gown and trowsers. The utility of the tread-wheel for the correction of offenders, has been for some time in use, not only in the mother country, but in some of the Colonies. It is stated to be the "terror of indolence, the reformer of vice, and the best moral preceptor as yet discovered for those proverbially desolate establishments, goals." We think, however, this new system of prison discipline ought to be dispensed with in all cases of female delinquency. Indeed it is revolting to every feeling of our nature to see women subject to torture and exposure of this nature.

September 2nd, 1828.

Bermuda Royal Gazette

(A Defence of Mary Prince's slaveowners,
Mr. & Mrs. John Wood)

Hamilton, November 22, 1831

THE ANTI-SLAVERY SOCIETY, AND THE
WEST INDIA COLONISTS.

One of the most important duties of the public press is the refutation of calumnies, and the protection of injured individuals or communities from slanderous and infamous attacks; and in no case are we called on more imperatively than we find ourselves to be on perusing a woman of colour named Mary Prince, who is falsely designated a *"West India Slave,"* but who is, in fact, a *free* woman residing in London. This pamphlet, to the extent of near fifty pages, is, with a deceptive mask, apparently issued under the authority of the secretary to the Anti-Slavery Society; who, there can be no doubt, felt ashamed to give the sanction of their name to procedure so stamped with falsehood and malignity, as to be disreputable to the character of any individual or association, much less of one *professing* charity and benevolence to all men. How an individual, holding the respectable situation which Mr. Pringle enjoys, that of *paid* secretary to the Anti-Slavery Society, could so far forget himself as to give credence and publicity to assertions not merely unsupported, but in *direct* variance with each other, and affording of themselves, a complete refutation, is indeed extraordinary; and we are the more disposed to wonder that any persons calling themselves gentlemen, could be guilty of publishing many thousand pamphlets of such testimony, against not merely a man of universally acknowledged high character, but also of making it a handle for grave and serious charges against the whole body of West India proprietors, whose reputation no means have been left untried to blacken and defame. We shall select this case of Mary Prince, so industriously circulated by Mr. Pringle, as a specimen of the mode in which the public mind in England is poisoned against their brethren in the West Indies. Our limits will not permit us to enter so fully into the case as it warrants, or as our inclination would prompt; we shall, however, give a brief abstract, premising that we know *nothing* of any of the parties, pro or con, in the affair; that we have been guided solely by the dictates of common justice, and that our statements in refutation, are drawn from the most incontrovertible testimony of the highest respectability in England and the West Indies, which are now in our possession, and which are open to the inspection of the Anti-Slavery Society at any moment.

Mr. Wood, a highly respectable merchant in Antigua, purchased many years ago, a slave, named Mary Prince, at Bermuda, who earnestly entreated him to buy her, and who, she confesses in her narratives "did not want to purchase her." Mr. Wood, however, at length relieved her from the miserable situation for which she states herself to have been, where she had been several times flogged, and the stripes of which, strange to say, have been insidiously preferred as charges *against* Mr. Wood, although he paid £67 sterling to relieve her! After living in Mr. Wood's family for 13 years, where, as will be seen, Mary Prince was treated with the utmost kindness, and on Mr. Wood preparing to come to England, she begged so hard to go with him and her mistress, Mr. Wood was induced to permit her, on her earnest entreaty that change of climate would benefit her health; and, as an encouragement for good behaviour, promised that she would be free on her return to Antigua. In England her conduct became unbearable; she refused to work—declared that the roast beef and veal, (which the other servants ate) furnished to her was *"horse flesh"*—that "she would not eat cold meat not being accustomed to it in Antigua;" and, after a variety of similar conduct, was at last told by her master, that if she would not alter her mode of proceedings, she must either return to Antigua, or, as she was *free in England,* she must leave his house, as he could not have the peace of his family daily disturbed by her. After a repetition of such behaviour, she at length left his house, taking with her several trunks of clothes, and about *forty* guineas in money, which she had saved in Mr. Wood's service.

The Anti-Slavery Society lent a not unwilling ear to the statement of this woman, and the result is the pamphlet before us, published under the editorship of their vilest description. His lady, if we were to believe Mary Prince's evidence, is a monster in human shape; and they are both, according to Mr. Pringle, hypocritical, tyrannical, and revengeful, to a degree hitherto unheard of among the human race. They are accused in this statement "of *caring nothing* about their slave, Mary Prince," who was left when ill, (which she says was for months and months, from the cruel treatment she received from her *former master,*) *"to lie in a little out-house* that was swarming with bugs and other vermin"—that her *"mistress did not take any trouble about her,"* and that she must have "lain and died there but for her neighbours;" that Mrs. Wood caused her to be flogged by *desiring* a magistrate to do so—that her master was angry with her for marrying—that he would not permit her to *buy her freedom in Antigua*—that he turned her *out of doors* in London, and that he was ever since *refused to sell her liberty.* On these charges, unsupported by *any evidence,* except that of "a character so thoroughly despicable and degraded, that he is known in Antigua by the name of the *Affidavit Maker,* he readily making affidavits at the rate of one dollar each," and bearing in the very pamphlet itself direct testimony to their untruth, Mr. Wood and the West India colonists are held up to the scorn of the whole world, as fiends guilty of every diabolical atrocity. If we were to quote the evidence before us in refuting these falsehoods, we should fill several numbers of our journal; as we before said, we content ourselves with an abstract from the pamphlet itself, from unbiassed witnesses, and from the testimony of those who could have had no possible motive for misstating facts.

Mr. Wood retained Mary Prince 13 years in his service, after paying £67 for her: he paid her in cash *ten guineas* a year—provided her with a house and two rooms, "very comfortable," connected by a covered in gallery with his own dwelling house; when she was sick, paid a doctor for attending her; and Mrs. Wood *herself* brought Mary her food—often bought chickens to make her broth when very ill—provided her with breakfast and dinner of the same kind of provisions as those consumed by her own family, (actually sent from their own table), with the addition of frequent gifts of the best wines and spirits—never was seen to punish *her* or *any* of his negroes;—always desired his servants and slaves to attend church, and recommended Mary Prince in particular for the religious instruction of the Rev. J. Curtin; provided her with clothes, equal in quality almost with those of his own lady, from whom she received, as several witnesses state, *"four* or *five* suits a year, *independent* of Christmas clothing; very good Irish linen; muslin to make gowns with; shoes for constant wear, and stockings." She was always so well dressed as to have been seen changing her clothes *three times* of a Sunday; according to her *own confession* she was enabled to earn at times to the extent of £30 by *taking in washing, by selling coffee, yams, and other provisions,* to the captains of ships; by buying hogs cheap on board ship, and after fattening them with her master's food, selling them for *double* the money (paid for them) on shore: inducing her to take a husband, (in the hope of reclaiming her from the immoral habits to which she was addicted, and which led her to commit the most disgraceful lascivious acts,) and for which her master was compelled to prevent her leaving the house after ten o'clock at night; a proceeding which this immaculate angel of the Anti-Slavery Society protested against, as she asserted "the night was her own time." But we are weary of refuting the calumnies put forth against the colonists by the most dissolute and abandoned characters, and by men whose total want of veracity and character is well known in the West Indies. Suffice it to say, that Mr. Wood has most justly refused to be ensnared to the trap laid for him, to induce him to *sell the freedom* of Mary Prince, who is already *at liberty* in England; and who, if Mr. Wood were to treat as a slave, by bargaining for her, would subject himself to the penalties of an act of Parliament, which contains a special clause against such proceeding. That Mary Prince is not detained from her native land, as evidence from the circumstance of Bermuda, and not Antigua, being her natal soil, and that Mary has not been kept from her husband, is also evident from the fact of her husband having *married again,* in her absence, and who, in one of his letters before us, states he would "never trouble his head, not quit his nativity, on any such *fool's errand,* as looking after his late wife, Mary Prince!"

We cannot omit briefly stating, that Mr. and Mrs. Wood, who are thus calumniated by the *hired advocate* of the Anti-Slavery Society, (who sees nothing but purity in a prostitute because she knew how and when to utter the name of the Deity, to turn up the whites of her eyes, and to make a perfect mockery of religion,) are described by the most respectable magistrates and members of council in Antigua, after *twenty years'* acquaintance, as standing as high as human beings can stand, for "humanity to their dependants, uprightness of conduct, and kind, as affectionate and exemplary parents." Mrs. Wood is spoken of (by the Rev. Mr. Curtin,) as "a lady of *very mild and available manners;* and it is solemnly asserted, that "Mary Prince had grossly misrepresented Mr. and Mrs. Wood, whom they can vouch for as being the most *benevolent and kind hearted* people that can possibly live!" The only Antigua evidence brought forth as to Mary Prince's character is that she was *decently and becomingly* dressed; why so was Mrs. Clarke, when she was visited by the Duke of York, yet no one would adduce that as a proof of Mrs. Clarke's reputation, except Mrs. Pringle, who is reluctantly and costively forced to admit, that Mary is of a *violent and hasty temper;*"—that she enjoys "a *considerable share of natural pride and self-importance;*" and that she does not even make a compensation for this as many domestics do, by being an *"expert servant."* We cannot omit the following testimony, which bears so irrefragably on the subject, and which is indeed but a brief portion of the evidence before us.

Extract of a letter of Dr. Chipman, dated Antigua, April 5, 1881:—
"The conduct of Mrs. Wood to the slaves about her is more that of the parent than the mistress ever attentive to their wants, her benevolence

and liberal charity to the poor of all classes and colours, ought never to be forgotten by the inhabitants of Antigua."

A letter from Dr. Nicholson states, "A short time before she left this country, Mrs. Wood consulted me about the propriety of taking Molly to England with her, stating that it was her own particular request, as she, (Molly) imagined that the change of climate would be of service to her complaints. I replied, that I could not coincide in opinion with Molly, that a change to a northern climate was likely to benefit a rheumatic affection; but as she had made a particular request, Mrs. Wood might use her own discretion—the change would at all events amuse her, and I did not conceive her complaints to be of such importance as to be materially injured by the measure.—Mrs. Wood acceded to her request, and thus concluded my acquaintance with Molly."

A letter from Dr. Weston states, (in reference to the slaves) "They were always comfortably lodged, clothed, and well fed; and whenever any of them were sick, no individuals from any quarter of the world could possible have evinced more tender feelings towards them than Mr. and Mrs. Wood; indeed, such was Mrs. Wood's anxiety and solicitude, in particular about the woman Molly, that whenever she was ill, my visits to her were, if anything, more frequent than most of the other slaves; being aware that it afforded Mrs. Wood considerable satisfaction and relief to her mind, as it appeared to me that Molly was more in the character of a confidential servant, and evidently was indulged to such an extent that often drew the attention of Dr. Coull and myself, more particularly as I always considered her to be of a morose and sullen disposition; and so far would she carry this, that at times it was a matter of some difficulty to ascertain what could please her."

It will, perhaps be not amiss if we give our readers the following queries which have been put to Molly's late husband, and his replies thereto; among other questions, he has been asked—

"Did I, (Mr. Wood,) ever punish Molly to your knowledge?—Never.

Did she live in a house of two rooms, immediately adjoining my own?—Yes.

Was this house comfortable; or was it full of vermin?—I never saw any vermin in it, and it was very comfortable.

Did not I tell you when you asked leave to visit the house, it was long my wish that Molly should take a husband, and although a free man, I will protect you and treat you well, while your conduct merited it?—You did.

Do you know that she had a considerable sum of money, and do you know that she lent the white cooper, Burchell, money, which I obliged him to pay her?—I did not know at the time I took up with her that she had lent any money, but she afterwards told me of it, and as I could not get it from Mr. Burchell I advised her to tell you of it, which she did, and you got it from him."

We take our leave of this disgusting conduct, which goes far to compromise the character of a society, which numbers many eminent and worthy individuals among its members, be warning the public to receive with doubt, and indeed with distrust, statements coming from a quarter so jaundiced on a great public question, which equally concerns the welfare of masters and slaves.—*United Kingdom.*

An Excerpt from the *Royal Gazette*

(A contemporary update of James Macqueen's
19th-century views)

January 20, 1994

ROW OVER "BENIGN" SLAVERY COMMENT IN TOURIST BROCHURE

A row has broken out over a Government tourist brochure which says slavery was more gentle in Bermuda than in other places.

The new booklet, aimed at encouraging "cultural" visits, says the Island had a "relatively benign system of slavery."

Benign, says the Oxford dictionary, means gracious or gentle.

About 30,000 copies of the brochure have been printed by Tourism. The description of Bermuda's slave system comes under the heading "black history."

It was written, along with the rest of the booklet, by advertising writer Mr. Edward Bottone, known as the "Curious Cook" in his articles and TV shows.

"There was nothing benign about slavery in Bermuda," said historian and former PLP senator Mr. Ira Philip.

"Some of the most brutal measures were undertaken by the slave masters, by those who institutionalised slavery in Bermuda.

"It was as cruel and as degrading as anywhere in the world."

The Island's self-governing rulers "did as they liked," he said. And they set precedents with laws governing slaves.

"Some of the most brutal punishments were inflicted on slaves for the slightest deviation from those regulations."

Youth Library head Mrs. Florence Maxwell said she also objected to the "relatively benign" phrase.

"Slavery nowhere was benign. Here it was equally as brutal and as cruel."

This was clear from the life story of Bermudian slave Mary Prince.

"Her book was only introduced to Bermudians very recently. It's a horror story. No slave ever was happy about their lot in life.

"For some strange reason Bermuda has never dealt with slavery honestly, maybe because the Island is small and there's a lot of guilt.

"It's got to be dealt with. It's history and we can't pretend it didn't happen, or it was a Sunday School picnic."

But cultural commentator Mr. Andrew Trimingham defended the brochure's statement.

"I'm not defending the institution of slavery but I think it's a true comment.

"The nasty slavery was associated with plantations. We didn't have plantations or anything resembling plantations.

"The slaves that we had were either domestics or subsistence farmers.

"They must have been quite remarkably well treated because they were crews for our ships.

"The ships were sailed by a small team and it can only have worked when master and slave were working together.

"There would have been exceptions to the generally benign system. But Bermuda's slave population was in the great part very, very fortunate compared to the appalling experience that their fellows down south had to try to survive.

"Very broadly they were not treated like chattels here, they were treated like people."

Historian Mr. William Zuill said: "To my mind, what was said by a lady in 1828 seems to me to be correct. She said that slavery was a dreadful institution but that in Bermuda it wore its mildest face."

He thought the brochure should perhaps have used "comparatively" rather than "relatively."

"And it probably should have had something saying it was a dreadful institution and a dreadful way of treating people.

"There was a good deal of harshness and cruelty. But there were occasions when slave crews could have escaped from Bermuda and didn't."

Mr. Cyril Packwood, who has written a book on Bermudian slavery, was off the Island. Other experts declined to comment.

Mr. Bottone defended his choice of words. "From my reading and from what I could find, imported labour was relatively well treated.

"But my reading and my research could have been misleading because everyone writes history to their agenda."

There had been worse treatment in the US and Haiti, he said.

He had thought it important to raise the subject in the booklet.

"It's not to be ignored, or to be highlighted as something horrendous or heinous or something we should hang our heads in shame for.

"I think it's just part of the past and it should be studied along with the past. I don't think it's a hot issue.

"In those times these practices were accepted, however horrible they seem to be today."

Tourism Minister the Hon. C. V. (Jim) Woolridge said he did not want to get involved in a row.

"If we dwell on these subjects we create ongoing controversy. I'm trying to give tourism a positive direction and I think that's what this brochure is doing."

A Second Excerpt from the *Royal Gazette*

January 21, 1994

COMPLAINTS CAUSE NEW TOURISM
BROCHURE TO BE WITHDRAWN

Government last night scrapped a new tourist brochure after complaints that it played down the suffering of Bermudian slaves.

Tourism officials will print a new version, costing taxpayers an estimated five-figure sum.

About 30,000 copies of the brochure, already printed will be withdrawn.

The Government decision came hours after *The Royal Gazette* revealed the brochure's contents.

The booklet was aimed at tourists interested in Bermuda's heritage.

In a section on black history, it said the Island's system of slavery was "relatively benign."

Benign, says the Oxford dictionary, means gracious or gentle.

The description outraged some historians who said Bermudian slavery was as cruel as it was anywhere else. Other experts agreed with the brochure.

But yesterday acting Tourism Minister the Hon. Gerald Simons and Human Affairs Minister the Hon. Jerome Dill said it could clash with Government moves towards racial harmony.

"We fully understand why people would find the remark offensive," they said in a joint statement.

"It seems to us that whether slaves were treated well or badly in Bermuda is beside the point. Slavery is and always was dehumanising."

"Today, Bermuda's efforts to deal with the lingering social and racial problems generated by segregation will be easier if we look squarely at the historical fact of slavery."

The new Human Affairs department was trying to "develop positive relationships" among Bermudians.

"To detract from the debilitating character of slavery will be an impediment to this task."

"The purpose of this booklet is to sell Bermuda as a destination that has a strong heritage to offer."

"If the sentence is left as it is, it may be distracting."

"This is a mistake in a document designed to assist our tourism effort—we do not want to make some people more interested in debating the possibility of 'benign' slavery than in debating whether to come here."

Earlier this week, Tourism Minister the Hon. C. V. (Jim) Woolridge said he did not want to get involved in a row over the brochure.

"If we dwell on these subjects we create ongoing controversy," he said. "I'm trying to give tourism a positive direction and I think that's what this brochure is doing."

Yesterday the Ministers said they had spoken to Mr. Woolridge, who was in Germany, and he had agreed with them.

"He concurs, feeling the sentence was an unfortunate oversight."

The brochure was written by local advertising writer Mr. Edward Bottone, known as the "Curious Cook."

Proclamation in 1993

Order of Service Commemorating the Emancipation of Slaves in Bermuda (August 1, 1834) at The Dockyard Saturday, July 24, 1993 7:30 p.m. The Ministry of Community, Culture and Information
From The Premier On Behalf of The Bermuda Government
to Commemorate the Emancipation of All
Slaves in These Islands

WHEREAS, on August 28, 1833 H. M. King William IV with the advice and consent of the Imperial Parliament passes an Act for the Abolition of Slavery throughout the British Colonies; for promoting the industry of the Manumitted slaves; and for compensating the persons hitherto entitled to the services of such slaves and

WHEREAS, by Act No. 1 of 1834 of the Bermuda Parliament . . . it is expedient that an Act shall pass the Legislature . . . to effect the abolition of slavery . . . be it enacted that all and every person who, on the first day of August One thousand eight hundred and thirty-four shall be holden in Slavery within these Islands . . . be to all intents and purposes free and discharged of and from all manner of slavery and

WHEREAS, such persons shall be absolutely and forever manumitted and WHEREAS, the Children thereafter to be born to any such persons, and the offspring of such Children shall in like manner be free from their birth and

WHEREAS, from and after the said first day of August One thousand eight hundred and thirty-four, Slavery shall be and is hereby utterly and forever abolished and declared unlawful in these His Majesty's Islands of Bermuda and

WHEREAS, it is considered . . . that the Apprenticeship system . . . should be dispensed with . . . as respects these Islands.

NOW THEREFORE,

BE IT RESOLVED, that the people of Bermuda commemorate the abolition of slavery, the relieving of Free Blacks and Free persons of Colour from certain disabilities, liabilities and restrictions and the eventual enjoyment of rights, privileges and franchises.

AND, BE IT FURTHER RESOLVED, that this service function as a reminder of slavery which was a tragic example of man's inhumanity to man and may we pledge that such injustice and cruelty nevermore exist within our human experience. May we continually be reminded that where there is slavery there can be no freedom.

July 3, 1993   The Hon. Sir John Swan, K. B. E., J. P., M. P.

Vernon Jackson, *Paradise Found—Almost*

BUT WHO WAS CAPTAIN I——?

A search of records compiled by Genealogist Mrs. C. F. E. Hollis-Hallett shows that Captain I—— was Captain John Ingham who on September 26th, 1789 married Miss Mary Spencer Albuoy, both of Spanish Point; and on October 16th 1790 their son Benjamin (referred to by Mary as "Benjy") was born at Spanish Point. He was about two years younger than Mary Prince. Their house ("at the bottom of a very high hill") was probably at the bottom of Cox's Hill or Sandy Hill, and their farm was probably on the low, marshy land between Mills Creek and Woodlands Road, bordering the Pembroke Canal,—because "the cattle were staked about the pond side."

From Mrs. Hollis-Hallett's records I also found that in 1834 a man named Joseph Wood Ingham was the father of a female named Margaret Amelia PRINCE INGHAM.

I recently met a white Bermudian woman (of my age) who is a member of the Ingham family and now lives in Canada. She told me that for many years her family owned and operated a farm with dairy animals in the same area where Captain John Ingham had operated his farm. She related how on a Sunday morning in the early 1920s her family moved from Pembroke West to a farm in Smith's Parish. On that morning all the farm animals and dairy cattle were driven along the public road to

---

Paradise Found—Almost (Bermuda: Globe Press, 1994), 67–68.

their new location. We did not mention or discuss Captain John Ingham, but I would not be surprised if they were related.

And then there are the Inghams of "Ingham Vale" and surrounding areas at Cox's Hill who have been entrenched there for many long years. I'll bet they have an interesting tale to tell, if they know their family's history.

Bibliography

PRIMARY SOURCES

Devonshire Parish Assessment Books, located in Bermuda Archives, Government Administration Building, Parliament Street, Hamilton, Bermuda.

Devonshire Parish Records for 1798–1839, located in Bermuda Archives, Government Administration Building, Parliament Street, Hamilton, Bermuda.

Early Bermuda Wills 1629–1835, located in Bermuda Archives, Government Administration Building, Parliament Street, Hamilton, Bermuda.

General Index of Manumissions and Bills of Sale of Slaves Contained in Books of Miscellanies, located in Bermuda Archives, Government Administration Building, Parliament Street, Hamilton, Bermuda.

Index of Slave Names, located in Bermuda Archives, Government Administration Building, Parliament Street, Hamilton, Bermuda.

Ferguson, Moira. Introduction to *The History of Mary Prince, a West Indian Slave, Related by Herself,* by Mary Prince. Ann Arbor: University of Michigan Press, 1992.

Ingram, K. E., comp. *Source for West Indian Studies: A Supplementary Listing, with particular Reference to Manuscript Sources.* Switzerland: Inter Documentation Co Ag Zug, 1983.

Jackson, Vernon. *Paradise Found—Almost.* Bermuda: Globe Press, 1994.

Jacobs, Harriet [Linda Brent]. *Incidents in the Life of a Slave Girl.* San Diego, New York, London: Harcourt Brace Jovanovich, 1973.

Prince, Mary. Mary Prince's Petition. See Appendix 1 of this volume.

———. Postscript to the second edition of *The History of Mary Prince.* See Appendix 2 of this volume.

———. Appendix to the third edition of *The History of Mary Prince.* See Appendix 3 of this volume.

Pringle, Thomas. *Narrative of a Residence in South Africa. A New*

Edition. *To Which is Prefixed a Biographical Sketch of the Author by Josiah Conder.* London: Edward Moxon, 1840.
United Kingdom. *Hansard Parliamentary Debates,* Commons, 3d ser.,
vols. 1–3 (1830–31). Entry under "Slavery" in no. 11. n. p.
Wilkinson, Henry C. *Bermuda from Sail to Steam: The History of the
Island from 1784–1901.* London: Oxford University Press,
1973.

SECONDARY SOURCES

Books and Periodicals

Alexander, Ziggi, and Audrey Dewjee, eds. *Wonderful Adventures of
Mrs Seacole in Many Lands.* Bristol: Falling Wall Press, 1984.
Andrews, William L. *To Tell a Free Story: The First Century of Afro-
American Autobiography, 1760–1865.* Urbana and Chicago:
University of Illinois Press, 1986.
Athenaeum Journal of Literature, Science, and the Fine Arts. London,
Jan.–Dec., 1831.
Ballstadt, Carl, Elizabeth Hopkins, and Michael Peterman, eds. *Susanna
Moodie: Letters of a Lifetime.* Toronto: University of Toronto
Press, 1985.
———. *Letters of Love and Duty: The Correspondence of Susanna and
John Moodie.* Toronto: University of Toronto Press, 1993.
Beckles, Hilary McD. *Natural Rebels: A Social History of Enslaved
Black Women in Barbados.* New Brunswick and New Jersey:
Rutgers University Press, 1989.
Bush, Barbara. *Slave Women in Caribbean Society 1650–1838.* Bloo-
mington: Indiana University Press, 1990.
Butterfield, Stephen. *Black Autobiography in America.* Amherst: Univer-
sity of Massachusetts Press, 1974.
Craton, Michael. *Testing the Chains: Resistance to Slavery in the British
West Indies.* Ithaca, NY: Cornell University Press, 1982.
Critchley, Macdonald, ed. *Butterworth's Medical Dictionary.* 2d edi-
tion. London: Butterworth, 1978.
Curtin, Phillip D. *Africa Remembered: Narratives by West Africans
from the Era of the Slave Trade.* Madison: University of Wiscon-
sin Press, 1967.
Doyle, John Robert, Jr. *Thomas Pringle.* New York: Twayne, 1972.
Eaton, Sara. *Lady of the Backwoods: A Biography of Catherine Parr
Traill.* Toronto, Montreal: McClelland & Stewart, 1969.

Edinburgh Literary Journal or Weekly Register of Criticism and Belles Lettres. Edinburgh, Jan–June, 1831.

Edwards, Bryan. *The History, Civil and Commercial, of the British Colonies in the West Indies*. 2 vols. London, 1793.

Ferguson, Moira. *Subject to Others: British Writers and Colonial Slavery, 1678–1834*. New York: Routledge, 1992.

Fisher, Dexter, and Robert B. Stepto, eds. *Afro-American Literature: The Reconstruction of Instruction*. New York: Modern Language Association, 1979.

Foster, Frances Smith. *Witnessing Slavery: The Development of Ante-Bellum Slave Narratives*. Westport, CT, and London: Greenwood Press, 1979.

Freud, Anna. *The Ego and the Mechanisms of Defense*. New York: International Universities Press, 1966.

Freud, Sigmund. *Psychopathology of Everyday Life*. Vol. 6 of *Standard Edition of the Complete Psychological Works of Sigmund Freud*. Ed. James Strachey with Anna Freud. New York: Avon, 1965.

Fryer, Peter. *Staying Power: The History of Black People in Britian*. London and Sydney: Pluto Press, 1974.

Gates, Henry Louis, Jr. Introduction to *Our Nig: or Sketches from the Life of a Free Black*, by Harriet E. Wilson. London: Allison & Busby, 1984.

Goveia, Elsa V. *Slave Society in the British Leeward Islands at the End of the Eighteenth Century*. New Haven, CT: Yale University Press, 1965.

Hallett, C. F. E. Hollis. *Bermuda Index 1784–1914: An Index of Births, Marriages, Deaths, as Recorded in Bermuda Newspapers*. Vol. 2. Juniperhill Press.

Hayward, Walter Brownell. *Bermuda Past and Present: A Descriptive and Historical Account of the Somers Islands*. New York: Dodd, Mead & Co., 1911.

Hegel, G. W. F. *Phenomenology of Spirit*. Translated by A. V. Miller. Oxford: Clarendon Press, 1977.

Hobsbawm, Eric J. *Industry and Empire*. London: Penguin Books, 1968.

Hull, Gloria T., Patricia Bell Scott, and Barbara Smith, eds. *All the Women Are White, All the Blacks Are Men, but Some of Us Are Brave: Black Women's Studies*. New York: Feminist Press, 1982.

James, C. L. R. *The Black Jacobins: Toussaint L'Ouverture and the San Domingo Revolution*. London: Secker & Warburg, 1938.

Jekyll, Joseph, ed. *Letters of the Late Ignatius Sancho, an African*. London, 1782.

Kennedy, Jean. *Isle of Devils: Bermuda under the Somers Island Co.*

1609–1685. Hamilton, Bermuda: Collins in association with Baster's, 1971.

Kojève, Alexandre. *Introduction to the Reading of Hegel. Lectures on the Phenomenology of Spirit Assembled by Raymond Queneau.* Edited by Allen Bloom and translated by James H. Nichols. New York: Basic Books, 1969.

Lanaghan, Frances. *Antigua and the Antiguans: A Full Account of the Colony and its Inhabitants From the Time of the Caribs to the Present Day, Interspersed with Anecdotes and Legends. Also, an Impartial View of Slavery and the Free Labour Systems: The Statistics of the Island, and Biographical Notices of the Principal Families.* London: Saunders & Otley, 1844.

Lefroy, J. H. *Memorials of the Discovery and Early Settlement of the Bermudas or Somers Islands 1515–1685.* 2 vols. Bermuda Government Library, 1932.

Lerner, Gerda. *Black Women in White America: A Documentary History.* New York: Vintage Books, 1973.

Lorimer, Douglas. *Colour, Class and the Victorians: English Attitudes to the Negro in the Mid-Nineteenth Century.* Leicester and New York: Leicester University Press and Holmes & Meier, 1978.

Mathurin, Lucy. *The Rebel Woman in the British West Indies during Slavery.* Published by the Institute of Jamaica for the African-Caribbean Institute of Jamaica: Kingston, 1975.

Meiring, Jane. *Thomas Pringle: His Life and Times.* Cape Town, South Africa, and Amsterdam: Balkema, 1968.

Moodie, Susanna. *Roughing It in the Bush* or *Life in Canada.* Ed. Carl Ballstadt. Ottawa: Carleton University Press, 1988.

Moody, William, and Frederic Robinson. *Reports of Cases Determined at Nisi Prius, in the Courts of King's Bench, Common Pleas, and Exchequer, and on the Northern and Western Circuits, from the Sittings after Michaelmas Term, 1 Will. IV. 1830, Sittings after Trinity Term, 7 Will. IV. 1836, Inclusive.* London: Saunders & Benning, and J. and W. T. Clarke, 1837; *The English Reports,* vol. 174, *Nisi Prius 5.* London: W. Green; Edinburgh: Stevens & Sons, 1929.

Morton, A. L. *A People's History of England.* New York: International Publishers, 1938.

Okihiro, Gary, Y. *In Resistance: Studies in African, Caribbean, and Afro-American History.* Amherst: University of Massachusetts Press, 1986.

Oliver, Vere Langford. *The History of the Island of Antigua, One of the Leeward Caribbees in the West Indies. From the First Settlement in 1635 to the Present Time*. London: Mitchell and Hughes, 1894.

Packwood, Cyril Outerbridge. *Chained on the Rock: Slavery in Bermuda*. New York: Eliseo Torres; Bermuda: Baxter's Limited, 1975.

Phillips, Joseph. *West Indian Question: The Outline of a Plan for the Total, Immediate, and Safe Abolition of Slavery Throughout the British Colonies*. London: J. & A. Arch, 1833.

The Poetical Works of Thomas Pringle. With a Sketch of his life by Leigh Ritchie. London: Edward Moson, 1838.

Pope-Hennessy, Una Constance Birch. *Agnes Strickland, Biographies of the Queens of England, 1796–1874*. London: Chatto & Windus, 1940.

Pringle, Thomas. *His Life, Times, and Poems*. Cape Town: J. C. Juta, 1912.

Rawson, Mary Anne, comp. *The Bow in the Cloud; or, The Negro's Memorial. A collection of original contributions, in prose and verse, illustrative of the evils of slavery, and commemorative of its abolition in the British Colonies*. Jackson and Walford, 1834.

Riddell, Maria. *Voyages to the Madeira and Leeward Caribbean Isles: With Sketches of the Natural History of These Islands*. Edinburgh: Peter Hill; London: T. Cadell, 1792.

Robinson, Kenneth Ellsworth. *The Berkeley Educational Society's Origins and Early History*. Pembroke, Bermuda: Berkeley Educational Society, 1962.

———. *Heritage: Including an Account of Bermudian Builders, Pilots and Petitioners of the early Post-Abolition Period 1834–1859*. Hamilton, Bermuda, and London: Macmillan Education, Berkeley Educational Society, 1979.

Robinson, William H. *Phillis Wheatley and Her Writings*. New York and London: Garland, 1984.

Rogers, J. A. *Sex and Race: A History of White, Negro, and Indian Miscegenation on the Two Americas*. New York: J. A. Rogers, n.d.

Senior, Olive. *Working Miracles: Women's Lives in the English-Speaking Caribbean*. London: James Currey, 1991.

Shyllon, Folaris. *Black People in Britain 1555–1833*. London, New York, Ibadan: Oxford University Press for the Institute of Race Relations, 1977.

———. *Black Slaves in Britain*. London: Oxford University Press, 1974.

Smith, James E. *Slavery in Bermuda*. New York: Vantage Press, 1976.

Strickland, Agnes. *Lives of the Queens of England*. 12 vols. London: Henry Colburn, 1840–48.

Strickland, Susanna. *Enthusiasm: and Other Poems.* London: Smith, Elder, & Co., 1831.

Thomis, Malcolm I., and Jennifer Grimmett. *Women in Protest 1800–1850.* New York: St Martin's Press, 1982.

Thomson, David. *England in the Nineteenth Century.* Baltimore, MD: Penguin, 1950.

The Tourist: a Literary and Anti-Slavery Journal. Under the Superintendance of the Agency Anti-Slavery Society. London: John Crisp, 1833.

Tucker, Terry. *Beware the Hurricane! The Story of the Gyratory Tropical Storms That Have Struck Bermuda and the Islanders' Folk-Lore Regarding Them.* Hamilton: Bermuda Historical Society, Occasional Publication no. VIII.

Verrill, Addison E. *The Bermuda Islands.* New Haven, Conn.: Published by the Author, 1907.

Walton, John, Paul B. Beeson, and Ronald Bodley Scott, eds. *The Oxford Companion to Medicine,* vol. 2 Oxford: Oxford University Press, 1986.

Wilkinson, Henry C. *Bermuda from Sail to Steam: The History of the Island from 1784–1901.* 2 vols. London: Oxford University Press, 1973.

Williams, Eric. *Capitalism and Slavery.* New York: Capricorn Books, 1944.

Zuill, William. *Bermuda Sampler 1815–1850. Being a Collection of Newspaper Items, Extracts from Books and Private Papers, together with many Explanatory Notes and a Variety of Illustrations.* Bermuda: Bermuda Book Stores, 1937. Reprint, Bungay, Suffolk: Richard Clay & Son, n.d.

Zuill, W. S. *The Story of Bermuda and Her People.* London: Macmillan, 1973.

SECONDARY SOURCES

Articles

Bush, Barbara. " 'The Family Tree Is Not Cut': Women and Cultural Resistance in Slave Family Life in the British Caribbean," in Gary Okihiro, *In Resistance.*

———. "White Ladies, Coloured 'Favorites' and Black 'Wenches': Some Considerations on Sex, Race and Class Factors in Social Relations in the British Caribbean," *Slavery and Abolition: A*

Journal of Comparative Studies, vol. 2, no. 3 (December 1987) London: Frank Cass.

Caspar, David Barry. "The Antiguan Slave Conspiracy of 1736: A Case Study of the Origins of Collective Resistance." *William and Mary Quarterly* 35 (April 1978).

Craton, Michael. "Hobbesian or Panglossian? The Two Extremes of Slave Conditions in the British Caribbean 1781–1834." *William and Mary Quarterly* 35 (1978).

Craven, Wesley Frank. "An Introduction to the History of Bermuda." *William and Mary Quarterly* 17 (April 1937); (July 1937); 18 (January 1938).

Davis, Angela. "Reflections on the Black Women's Role in the Community of Slaves." *Black Scholar* (December 1971).

Ebbin, Meredith. "Gladys Misick Morrell and the Women's Suffrage Movement." *Bermudian* (May 1991).

"Generations in Business, Trimingham's—Established 1842." *Royal Gazette Special Supplement,* August 29, 1959.

Grant, Joan. "Call Lord: The History of Mary Prince," *Trouble and Strife* 14 (Autumn), 1988.

Gwin, Minrose C. "Green-Eyed Monsters of the Slavocracy: Jealous Mistresses in Two Slave Narratives." In *Conjuring: Black Women, Fiction, and Literary Tradition,* edited by Marjorie Pryse and Hortense J. Spillers.

Higman, B. W. "The Slave Populations of the British Caribbean: Some Nineteenth-Century Variations." *Eighteenth Century Florida and the Caribbean.* Ed. Samuel Proctor. Gainesville: University Press of Florida, 1976.

Leseur, H. A. "Richard Darrell—Patriarch of Hamilton." *Royal Gazette Special Supplement,* August 29, 1959.

Macqueen, James. "The Colonial Empire of Great Britain. Letter to Earl Grey, First Lord of the Treasury, etc., etc., for James Macqueen, esq." *Blackwood's Magazine* (November 1983).

McPhee, Robin. "And Every Tribe Shall Build One" Old Devonshire Church, Bermuda. *Bermudian* (May 1991).

Trimingham, Andrew. "All the Way to Crow Lane Side: Nothing There but Foolish Pride. A Quick Look at the Birth, Life and Death of Paget 'Society'." *Bermudian* (May 1991).

Zuill, William. "The Anti-Slavery Society, and the West Indian Colonists." *Bermuda Royal Gazette* (November 1831).